W9-COT-783

ESSAYS AND STUDIES
1971

ESSAYS AND STUDIES
1971

BEING VOLUME TWENTY-FOUR OF THE NEW SERIES
OF ESSAYS AND STUDIES COLLECTED FOR
THE ENGLISH ASSOCIATION

BY BERNARD HARRIS

NEW YORK: HUMANITIES PRESS

© The English Association 1971

Printed in Great Britain

391–00184–1

Contents

The Style of Wyatt's 'The Quyete of Mynde'

A. N. BRILLIANT

In 1527 Catherine of Aragon asked Wyatt to translate for her the second part of Petrarch's treatise *De Remediis Utriusque Fortunae*. Wyatt, finding the text tedious and repetitive, turned his attention instead to a very much shorter essay on the same topic by Plutarch, which he read in the Latin version (*De Tranquillitate et Securitate Animi*) of Guillaume Budé. He was able to present his completed translation of *The Quyete of Mynde* to the Queen on the last day of the year as a New-Year's gift.

Although this decision to render a different work from that requested by Catherine is most simply explained by comparing their relative lengths, Wyatt naturally having desired to relieve himself from what would have been a formidable and probably unrewarding labour, the choice is also of some relevance to an understanding of Wyatt's relation to the contemporary Humanist background. More than his obvious boredom with the Petrarch might at first suggest, the change of text represents a choice of style that reflects, if unconsciously, a whole body of classical and Renaissance theorizing about the kinds of language appropriate to a serious moral discourse. This body of theory is equally applicable to a consideration of the three satires or verse epistles.

Wyatt, by way of offering his excuses to the Queen, makes quite clear his reasons for finding *De Remediis* dull and intractable material:

The booke of Fraunces Petrarch/ of the remedy of yll fortune/ at the commaundement of your highnesse/ I assayd/ as my power wold serve me/ to make into our englyssh. And after I had made a profe of nyne or ten Dialogues/ the labour began to seme tedious/ by superfluous often rehersyng of one thyng. which

tho paraventure in the latyn shalbe la[u]dable/ by plentuous
diversite of the spekyng of it (for I wyll nat that my jugement
shall disalowe in any thyng so aproved an auctour) yet for
lacke of suche diversyte in our tong/ it shulde want a great dele
of the grace.[1] (sig. a. ii[r])

De Remediis is indeed an exhaustive work, and Wyatt was not
exaggerating Petrarch's repetitiveness. Divided into two parts, the
first comprises one hundred and twenty-two dialogues in which
Reason lectures Joy and Hope on the wisdom of detachment from
the smiles of a deceptive and fickle fortune. Book Two—'of the
remedy of yll fortune'—consists of a further one hundred and
thirty-two dialogues, with Reason now urging upon Sorrow and
Fear a Christian and Stoic fortitude before the buffets of adversity.
The message of the whole is contained in the advice: 'Spernere
mundum, spernere nullum, spernere sese, se sperni, hoc tibi
ultimo opus est'.[2] But, as Patricia Thomson has pointed out,[3]
already by the third dialogue of Book One Reason is more or less
admitting having nothing new to say: 'Quicquid de forma modo
diximus, repetitum puta'. *De Remediis* is a thoroughly medieval
work in its form, in its theme *de contemptu mundi* (the name of
another of Petrarch's treatises), and in its mood of profound pessi-
mism and monkish misanthropy. That Lydgate found it useful as
an authority in compiling his *Fall of Princes* seems entirely
appropriate.

Whether or not his ostensible reason for rejecting Petrarch's
text—that English would have been inadequate to the rhetorical
expansiveness of the Latin original—was primarily a pretext for
evading an unpalatable task, Wyatt's observations on the relative
copiousness and potential variety of the two languages are consistent with his immediately subsequent remarks on the qualities
that made Plutarch more attractive:

Altho/ as me semeth/ and as sayth this Plutarch/ the plentuous-

[1] All quotations from *The Quyete of Mynde* are taken from *Collected Poems of
Sir Thomas Wyatt*, edd. Muir and Thomson (Liverpool, 1969), pp. 440–63.
[2] *De Rem. Opera Omnia* (Basle, 1581), II. 36.
[3] *Sir Thomas Wyatt and his Background* (London, 1964), p. 81.

nesse and faire diversyte of langage/ shulde nat so moch be
desyred in suche thynges/ as the frutes of the advertysmentes
of them/ whiche in my opinyon/ this sayde Plutarch hath
handsomly gadred togyder/ without tedyousnesse of length/
contayning the hole effect/ of that your hyghnes desyred of
Petrarch in his lytell boke/ which he wrate to one of his frendes/
of the Quiete of mynde/ nerawhyt erryng from the purpose
of the sayd Petrarch. (sig. a. ii ʳ⁻ᵛ)

Petrarch's 'purpose' doubtless had more to do with 'the plentuousnesse and faire diversyte of langage' than Wyatt acknowledges
with that 'nerawhyt erryng' (just as, it will presently be argued,
Wyatt's intentions as a translator have to do with putting a particularly high premium on 'the frutes of the advertysementes'—
that is, the content—of his text). But Plutarch's subject is indeed
similar to that of *De Remediis*, though, less gloomy in mood and
less eschatological in tendency, he does offer a somewhat different
comfort against tribulation from Petrarch's. *De Tranquillitate
Animi* savours more of robust, rather trite good sense in counting
blessings and not crying over spilt milk than of total contemptuous
rejection of worldly things. In its practicality as in its empiricism,
for reason and nature are seen to teach wisdom through precept
and concrete example, the work is Erasmian. Where Petrarch had
advised that, since the wages of all terrestrial life are death, the sin
of discontent is no proper preparation for that end, Plutarch
diagnoses the *folly* of not being comforted. Quiet of mind is as
desirable for living as for dying.

It is, however, stylistically that Wyatt's translation proves most
thought-provoking. Immediately striking to the modern reader
are the unadorned directness and conciseness of the prose. Often
plain to the point of harshness or laconic to the point of obscurity
as it is, these features by no means necessarily make for simplicity
or fluency of thought:

Altho (for we ar now come to that madnesse/ that eche of our
lyves hangeth upon other mens/ more than our own/ and that
our nature is so altred/ in to a certeyn unkynde and envyous
affectyon/ nat so moch to glad in our owne/ as to be troubled

with other folkes welthes) if thou loke nat only upon those
wonders/ and famous thynges in them/ whom thou wenest very
blessed/ & (as they say) in Jovis lap/ but the curten & the fayr
travers drawen/ lettyng passe their glory and utter apparence/ if
aswell thou loke with in them/ thou shalt truly fynde many
inwardes/ sower & troblous. Pyttacus/ whom the sure fame
noyseth to have ben endewed with wysdome/ fortitude/ and
justyce/ whan he was chering gestes that he had/ it is sayd his
wyfe came and angerly overthrew the table wherwith whan he
sawe his gestes abasshed eche of you/ quoth he/ is troubled with
some yll/ I am in this state alway very well. This man that was
demed abrode to be very happy/ whan so ever he entred his
threshold/ he semed to be a wretch/ I say nat that he was one/
where his wyf had all and ruled princely/ where oftimes &
alway he neded to fyght with her. Many thynges do trouble
you/ nothyng dothe trouble me. Many such lyke thinges do
cleve unto glory/ unto riches/ ye and unto a kyngdome. but
truely of the ignorant multytude unperceyved/ for the pompe is
drawen/ behynde the which those thinges lye hydden. (sig. b.
vi^v–vii^r)

It will, I suppose, be readily conceded that this prose is not distinguished for elegance or lucidity. The loose syntax—each sentence primitive in structure yet involutedly struggling with an
unwieldy rush of minor clauses, the irregular punctuation, the
confused metaphor of the drawn curtain—these are characteristic
defects of *The Quyete of Mynde*.

On the positive side is the simple dignity often achieved by
Wyatt's plain diction and direct manner; what he wants in grace
is at times compensated by a dignified forthrightness or a sudden
vivid phrase. The closing sentences are representative of the re-
strained eloquence lurking just beneath the rather flat surface:

And yet most unsely is this/ whan we delyte in orgaynes played
and sounded/ and in lytell byrdes songes/ and beholde gladly the
beestes playng and daunsyng/ and agayne ar offended with their
frowarde noyse and their cruell lokes/ yet neverthelesse seyng
our owne lyves sadde and hevy/ frownyng/ & overthrowen with
most troublous affections and tangled busynesses/ and cures/ and

driven with untemperatnesse/ that nat only we can nat gette us
some lyberte and space to take our brethe/ but nother here also
other exhortyng us to it. To whose warnynges with clere and
opyn eares/ if we wolde gyve hede/ we shulde use thinges
present as they come without any blame/ and shulde rest with
the plesaunt remembraunce of thynges past/ and at the last
we shulde drawe towarde thynges to come/ unferefully and
assuredly/ with sure and gladsome shyning hope. (sig. d. iii^v–iv^r)

Even here Wyatt's brevity, when compared with the ease of
Thomas Blundeville in his version (1561) or Philemon Holland's
more aureate mannerisms in his (1603),[1] appears précis-like and
halting. But Wyatt's shortness never blurs and weakens the stark-
ness of Plutarch's stoic message, as is frequently the case with
Holland's habitual doubling of words and overall prolixity.

That this short, hard style would have been difficult going for
the contemporary reader of *The Quyete of Mynde* is clear from the
Preface (either by Wyatt or by Richard Pynson, the printer) 'To
the reder':

It shall seme harde unto the paraventure gentyll reder/ this
translation/ what for shorte maner of speche/ and what for
dyvers straunge names in the storyes. As for the shortnesse
advyse it wele and it shalbe the plesaunter/ whan thou under-
standest it. (sig. ai^v.)

That, as it stands, might sound like special pleading—an attempt to
divert the reader from finding the translation incompetent by
asking him to do all the work. But Wyatt indicates that a 'shorte
maner of speche' was adopted deliberately when he says in his
Dedication that he was 'seking rather the profite of the sentence
than the nature of the wordes', a formula he derived from
Plutarch's own introductory remark to Paccius, the addressee of

[1] 'The Port of Rest', *Three Morall Treatises* set forth by Tho. Blundeville
(London, 1580), sig. e. i^r – h. vii^v.
    'Of the Tranquillity and contentment of Minde', *The Philosophie, commonlie
called, The Morals*, Philemon Holland (London, 1603), pp. 144–62.
    For comparisons of the prose in these translations with Wyatt's see Thomson,
op. cit., pp. 103–7, and Muir, *Life and Letters of Sir Thomas Wyatt* (Liverpool,
1963), pp. 11–12.

the essay, that 'thou sekes nat the delicacy of sayeng/ and the piked delight of spech/ and thou hast consyderatyon onely of some doctryne/ to be as helpe for the lyfe to be ordered' (a. iii^v). From these hints we can infer that Wyatt was not shirking but taking up a distinct and consistent attitude in opposing Petrarch's 'plentuousnesse and faire diversyte of langage' to 'the frutes of the advertysmentes'.

We can get some idea of the significance of this attitude from a passage of criticism written about a century later, but borrowed from a writer who was contemporary with Wyatt. Ben Jonson, paraphrasing Vives, has the following to say on contracted styles:

> Wee must expresse readily, and fully, not profusely. There is difference betweene a liberall, and a prodigall hand. As it is a great point of Art, when our matter requires it, to enlarge, and veere out all sayle; so to take it in, and contract it, is of no lesse praise when the Argument doth aske it. Either of them hath their fitnesse in the place. . . . A strict and succinct style is that, where you can take away nothing without losse, and that losse to be manifest. The briefe style is that which expresseth much in little. The concise style, which expresseth not enough, but leaves somewhat to bee understood. The abrupt style, which hath many breaches, and doth not seeme to end, but fall.[1]

Just where the prose of *The Quyete of Mynde* lies on this scale of conciseness is debatable; the close connection between Wyatt's profession of intent, the style of the end-product, and the kinds of manner Jonson is there describing, is manifest. To the extent that it can be established that this connection is no coincidence, but reflects a similarity of stylistic outlook derivable from an identifiable critical tradition, the case for seeing some sort of continuity between Wyatt and Jonson makes sense.

Those remarks from the *Discoveries* are not isolated but form part of the statement of a total rhetorical position which has been thoroughly discussed by Wesley Trimpi in the first part of his book on *Ben Jonson's Poems*.[1] Trimpi relates this position to two

---

[1] *Timber: or, Discoveries; Ben Jonson*, edd. Herford and Simpson, VIII, p. 623.
[2] Stanford, 1962.

broad stylistic debates, the Asiatic–Attic controversy of antiquity
and the Ciceronian–Senecan controversy of the Renaissance, both
of which were substantially concerned with the stylistic characteristics appropriate to the moral discourse (*sermo*). These con-
troversies may in turn be related to the Socratic opposition of
rhetoric, associated with the sophists, whose purpose was to
persuade, to dialectic, which aimed at the discovery and dissem-
ination of the truth. In accordance with these differing ends there
were enlisted different types of expression; 'rhetoric', says Trimpi:

> claimed the high style, whose 'intention' or *officium* was to
> move (*movere*), and the middle style, whose purpose was to
> delight (*delectare*). Dialectic employed the plain style, whose
> *officium* was simply to teach (*docere*). The conflict between
> dialectic and rhetoric, which Plato discusses in the *Gorgias* and
> the *Phaedrus*, encouraged, in the most general terms, a split be-
> tween meaning and expression, between the philosopher and
> the orator, and between teaching and persuasion. Cicero
> blamed Socrates for the separation: 'This is the source [the
> composition of Plato] from which has sprung the undoubtedly
> absurd and unprofitable and reprehensible severance between
> the tongue and the brain, leading to our having one set of
> professors to teach us to think and another to teach us to speak'
> (*De Oratore* III. xvi. 61). Socrates made the separation in the
> name of philosophy; Cicero attempted to rejoin the two disci-
> plines in the creation of an ideal orator, but in doing so became a
> partisan of an oratorically ornate or 'Asiatic' style. He regarded
> the Socratic school as furnishing a model for the plain style,
> which was designated *sermo* or the conversational style.[1]

Perhaps the best description of the plain style, certainly one of the
most detailed, is provided by Cicero's own extended account, in
his *Orator*, of the so-called Attic exponent of the art:

> First, then, we must delineate the one whom some deem to be
> the only true 'Attic' orator. He is restrained and plain (*humilis*),

---

[1] p. 6. See also Morris W. Croll, '"Attic Prose" in the 17th century', *Studies
in Philology*, Vol. 18, 1921, pp. 79–128. Of the plain style generally Croll says
'the *genus* as a whole is properly charactized by its origin in *philosophy*' (p. 88).

he follows the ordinary usage (*consuetudinem imitans*), really differing more than is supposed from those who are not eloquent at all . . . For that plainness of style seems easy to imitate at first thought, but when attempted nothing is more difficult. [The style] should be loose but not rambling; so that it may seem to move freely but not to wander without restraint. He should also avoid, so to speak, cementing his words together too smoothly, for the hiatus and clash of vowels have something agreeable about it [sic] and show a not unpleasant carelessness on the part of a man who is paying more attention to thought than to words. But his very freedom from periodic structure and cementing his words together will make it necessary for him to look to the other requisites. For the short and concise clauses must not be handled carelessly, but there is such a thing even as a careful negligence. Just as some women are said to be handsomer when unadorned—this very lack of ornament becomes them—so this plain style gives pleasure even when unembellished: there is something in both cases which lends greater charm, but without showing itself. Also all noticeable ornament, pearls as it were, will be excluded; not even curling irons will be used; all cosmetics, artificial white and red, will be rejected; only elegance and neatness will remain. The language will be pure Latin, plain and clear; propriety will always be the chief aim. Only one quality will be lacking, which Theophrastus mentions fourth among the qualities of style—the charm and richness of figurative ornament. He will employ an abundance of apposite maxims dug out from every conceivable hiding place; this will be the dominant feature in this orator. He will be modest in his use of what may be called the orator's stock-in-trade. For we do have after a fashion a stock-in-trade, in the stylistic embellishments, partly in thought and partly in words.

. . . The orator of the plain style, provided he is elegant and finished, will not be bold in coining words, and in metaphor will be modest, sparing in the use of Archaisms, and somewhat subdued in using the other embellishments of language and of thought. Metaphor he may possibly employ more frequently because it is of the commonest occurrence in the language of townsman and rustic alike.

. . . As in the appointments of a banquet he will avoid extravagant display, and desire to appear thrifty, but also in good taste, and will choose what he is going to use. There are, as a matter of fact, a good many ornaments suited to the frugality of this very orator I am describing. For this shrewd orator must avoid all the figures that I described above, such as clauses of equal length, with similar endings, or identical cadences, and the studied charm produced by the change of a letter, lest the elaborate symmetry and a certain grasping after a pleasant effect be too obvious . . . But many of these figures of thought will be appropriate to this plain style, although he will use them somewhat harshly.

A speech of this kind should also be sprinkled with the salt of pleasantry, which plays a rare great part in speaking. There are two kinds, humour and wit . . .

For my part, I judge this to be the pattern of the plain orator —plain but great and truly Attic.[1]

Similar accounts of the plain style are to be found in Demetrius, Dionysius of Halicarnassus, Seneca, and Quintilian,[2] and in all these critics may be seen the foundations for much of what Jonson wrote in his *Discoveries*, often in straight translation. For example, the celebrated passage beginning 'Custome is the most certaine Mistresse of Language',[3] though taken from Quintilian (*Inst. Orat.* I. 6. 3), is the same in import as the first and third of the paragraphs quoted from Cicero above.

These classical formulations about Attic prose were taken up and developed in the Renaissance by Juan Luis Vives in his *De Ratione Dicendi* and *De Conscribendis Epistolis* and by Erasmus in *De Copia Verborum* and, again, *De Conscribendis Epistolis*. Vives contrasts

---

[1] *Orator*, pp. 75–90. Loeb trans.
[2] Demetrius, *On Style*, pp. 190–222, 223–40, 246–55.
Dionysius, *On Literary Composition* III.
Seneca, *Epistles* 40.
Quintilian, *Inst. Orat.* VIII. Preface 17–26, 2. 22–4; IX. 1. 17–19, 4. 19–21; X. 1. 44, 64–5; XII. 10. 16–80.
For other remarks by Cicero, see *Brutus* 119, 201 ff., 283 ff.; *Orator* 20 ff.; *De Orat* II. 80. 326 ff. Cf. also Horace *Sermones* I. 10. 9–15 ('. . . est brevitate opus, ut currat sententia neu se/ impediat verbis lassas onerantibus aures . . .') and *Epistulae* II. 2. 115–25.
[3] Loc. cit., VIII, p. 622.

the Att :tyle with the Asiatic, represented respectively by Seneca and by Cicero. Of the latter manner he says:

> The nerves a.c often buried by flesh and fat, so that they are weakened and are less able to perform their functions. It happens in the same way in style, that the luxuriance of words and the redundancy of flesh and that diffuse and wandering composition become responsible for a weak style, which happened to Cicero who, while he diluted his subject matter too much with words, lost strength, as a ri   that fl ws out widely.[1]

And the same distinction between functional plainness, using simple and direct language, and expansive embellishment, with the use of archaisms and neologisms, is central to the Humanist critique of style. The dichotomy is most succinctly summarized in English by the juxtaposition of Ascham's lament, 'Ye know not, what hurt ye do to learning, that care not for words, but for matter, and so make a devorse betwixt the tong and the hart',[2] with Bacon's (reiterated by Jonson), that the study of eloquence:

> grew speedily to an excess; for men began to hunt more after words than matter; and more after the choiceness of the phrase, and the round and clean composition of the sentence, and the sweet falling of the clauses, and the varying and illustration of their works with tropes and figures, than after the weight of matter, worth of subject, soundess of argument, life of invention, c depth of judgement . . . Here therefore [is] the first distemper of learning, when men study words and not matter.[3]

If we except from the accounts of the plain style the emphasis placed by the various classical and Humanistic critics on elegance, we are left with a full description of Wyatt's manner in *The Quyete of Mynde*. Each of Cicero's points in the quotation above has some bearing on Wyatt's prose, and the whole passage makes

[1] *De Rat. Dic.*, II, v; *Opera Omnia* (Valencia, 1782), II, p. 144. Trans. Trimpi, p. 54.
[2] *The Scholemaster* (1570), ed. J. E. B. Mayor (London, 1934), p. 181.
[3] *Advancemer f Learning*, Book I; *The Works of Francis Bacon*, edd. Spedding, Ellis and Heath (London, 1861), Vol. I pp. 283–4. See also *Discoveries*; loc. cit., VIII, p. 627.

abundantly clear the unsuitability of *De Remediis* as a model for a translator wishing to avoid the 'studied charm' of Petrarch's elaborately balanced structure, tireless repetition of themes, and diffuse luxuriance of language.[1] But hardness and obscurity are not qualities that figure in Cicero's exposition of Attic oratory, and it remains to be explained why Wyatt's conciseness so often leaves an impression of gracelessness and inelegance.

The explanation is not hard to find since these defects, the same critics all agree, are characteristic manifestation of those excesses to which the plain style, by virtue of its aim of not being too polished or too eager to charm, is particularly prone. In the catalogue of contracted styles which Jonson borrowed from Vives an indication has already been given of the range of concentration possible within Atticism or Senecanism. Elsewhere in the *Discoveries* Jonson is critical of the extremes to which the desire for succinctness may lead—as, for instance, when he lists the qualities necessary to the writing of letters:

> The next property of *Epistolarie* style is Perspicuity, and is often-times indangered by the former qualitie (brevity) . . . Few words they darken speech, and so doe too many: as well too much light hurteth the eyes, as too little . . .[2]

Beside this may be set Cicero's remarks on the 'Thucydideans':

> There are many kinds of Atticists: but these of our day apprehend the nature of one kind only. They think that the only one who attains the Attic norm is he who speaks in rough and unpolished style, provided only that he is precise and discriminating in thought . . . And here come some who take the title

---

[1] Cf. also Morris Cook, loc. cit., p. 92: 'The historian versed in the poetry of this period [late sixteenth century] can detect the coming of the severer air of the seventeenth century in the new distaste that declares itself everywhere for the copious and flowing style of Ariosto and Spenser, and the "tedious uniformity" of Petrarcanism.'

[2] Loc. cit., VIII, p. 631. 'Jonson here copies Hoskyns verbally, but Vives and Lipsius may have been in his mind, in view of the terseness with which he reproduces them as much as he does Seneca' (Herford and Simpson, XI, p. 278). Cf. also Horace, *Ars Poetica*, ll. 25–6: 'brevis esse laboro, obscurus fio'.

'Thucydideans' ... Those famous speeches [of 'Thucydides']
contain so many dark and obscure sentences as to be scarcely
intelligible ... Are men so perverse as to live on acorns after
grain has been discovered? ... No one, however, succeeds in
imitating his dignity of thought and diction, but when they
have spoken a few choppy, disconnected phrases ... each one
thinks himself a regular Thucydides.[1]

And Dionysius of Halicarnassus says of the same historian:

The most obvious of his characteristics is the attempt to indicate
as many things as possible in as few words as possible, to com-
bine many ideas in one, and to leave the listener expecting to
hear something more. The consequence is that brevity becomes
obscurity.[2]

The faults of style in *The Quyete of Mynde* stem more from primitive syntax than from complexity of ideas, but Wyatt undoubtedly
displays an unwillingness to expand the Latin he was working
from, as Blundeville and Holland did for the sake of clarity.

It should be noted, of course, that the brevity of the treatise is
not solely of Wyatt's design, but very much a part of his model. In
his introduction to the facsimile reprint[3] Professor Baskervill
speculates that 'Possibly Wyatt was trying to achieve the com-
pendiousness of Latin style through the structure of his English
sentences'; and the literalness of the translation certainly confirms
this. But however deliberately Wyatt was experimenting, it
should not be forgotten that Plutarch's own manner was noted for
its brevity:

For how harsh or rude soever my speech be, yet am I sure that
my translation will be much easier to my contriemen, than the
Greeke copie is, even to such as are best practised in the Greeke

---

[1] *Orator*, pp. 28–32. Loeb trans.

[2] *The Three Literary Letters*, ed. and trans. W. Rhys Roberts (Cambridge,
1901), pp. 133–7.

[3] *Quyete of Mynde* (1527), reproduced in facsimile, with introduction by C. R.
Baskervill (Cambridge, Mass., 1931).

tonge, by reason of Plutarkes peculiar maner of inditing, which is rather sharpe, learned, and short, than plaine, polished, and easie.[1]

On top of this came the mediation of Budé, whose 'dry erudition' Sandys contrasts with Erasmus's 'rich variety and . . . sparkling wit',[2] and of whom Ascham laconically jotted down:

> Budaeus in his Commentaries roughlie and obscurelie, after his kinde of writyng.[3]

Thus much of the difficulty of the translation is inherent in its sources, and not attributable to Wyatt. Nevertheless, his choice of sources, we have seen, was particularly deliberate, and everything points to this short, plain style's having been distinctly congenial to him.

Professor Baskervill also observes that Wyatt shows 'an evident interest in native English words and an avoidance of Latinized vocabulary'. Idiomatic vigour and a propensity for pithy proverbial phrasing are indeed Wyatt's great strength as a translator in *The Quyete of Mynde*, and numerous illustrations could be offered to demonstrate this most successful aspect of his wresting a natural, colloquial English from the Latin. Here are just a few examples:

(a) sore toos are nat esed with gorgious showes/ nor the whittlowe with a ring/ nor the hedach with a crowne. (a. iii^v)

(b) thou seest other mennes vices with kytes eyes/ & thyn own thou lettes passe/ with wynkynge owles eyes? (b. iii^r)

(c) thou canst nat shote an arowe with a plou/ or hunt an hare with an oxe/ . . . [or] hunt an hart with a dragge net. (b. vii^v)

(d) Surely we may stay forthwith ech misfortun/ I knew I had slypper riches/ nat nayled with sixe peny nayl/ as they say. (c. v^r)

---

[1] Plutarch, *Lives*, trans. North from Amyot's French (Oxford, 1928), Vol. I, pp. xxx–xxxi.
[2] *A History of Classical Scholarship*, J. E. Sandys (New York, 1964), Vol. II, p. 171.
[3] *The Scholemaster*, ed. cit., p. 189.

(*e*) For there is no speche that soner rebuketh thaffectionate parte of the mynde/ whan it is drawen overtwhartly with affections/ & whan it snatcheth the byt of reson in the teth/ than that that warneth us of our comen & naturall necessites/ unto whiche necessite man is borne . . . (c. vi^v)

(*f*) as tho he held the wolfe by the eres/ as the proverbe saith. (c. viii^r)

Cicero had advised his Attic orator, it will be remembered, to 'employ an abundance of apposite maxims dug out from every conceivable hiding place; this will be the dominant feature in this orator'. We can see the interest in *sententia* developed in the later writers, too; by example in the *Adagia* of Erasmus, by precept in Vives:

> Briefly, experience may be gained from all accounts of those things which are handed down as having been said or done, or, again, from those writings which have been composed and are suited to instruct men in wisdom. So, too, with adages and sentences, in a word, all those precepts of wisdom which have been collected from the observations of the wise, which have remained amongst the people, as if they were public wealth in a common storehouse.[1]

But here, too, Wyatt's own contribution is only partial, the chief impetus coming from his sources. While his choice of English idiom and vocabulary is impeccable, there has been no actual critical decision to introduce proverbial sayings and gnomic phrases. Of the six examples given above, two (*a* & *c*) are to be found in Plutarch's original. Although there is no sign in the Greek of the other four, we must not take Professor Muir's reminder that Wyatt 'is not afraid of homely proverbial phrases'[2] to mean that they are his own idea, deliberately interpolated to enliven the text. By going to Budé's Latin we can gauge Wyatt's unashamed literalness:

---

[1] *De Tradendis Disciplinis*, I. 5, trans. as *Vives: on Education*, Foster Watson (Cambridge, 1913), p. 39.
[2] *Life and Letters of Sir Thomas Wyatt*, p. 11.

(b) aliena vitia milvinis oculis cernis: tua vero transmittis noc-
tuinis & conniventibus?[1] (b. 2^v)

(d) . . . sciebam precarias me opes nec trabali clauo fixas (ut
aiunt). (d. 2^r)

(e) . . . & ut ita dicam rationis frena momordit . . . (d. 3^r)

(f) quasique lupum auribus teneret: (ut est in proverbio).[2] (d. 4^r)

Regarding this last proverb Tilley, after citing the almost inevitable source in Erasmus's *Adagia*, gives Sir Thomas Elyot's dictionary of 1538 as the first English usage.[3] Wyatt's is earlier, but
taken, as we see, straight from Budé.

However, just as a plain and unembellished style was both an
integral feature of his models and perfectly congenial to Wyatt,
so this pervasive use of proverb, while no innovation on his part,
came to him easily and naturally. The evidence is to be found
throughout his other writings; in the correspondence with his son,
in the diplomatic dispatches, in the great Defence—most of all in
the three satires. Indeed, a convincing measure of the usefulness of
The Quyete of Mynde to him as apprentice work is the fact that,
when he came to forge his own personal brand of *sermo*, he
chose to incorporate several idiomatic phrases borrowed from his
translation of the treatise:

We accuse wicked fortune and our desteny/ whan rather we
shulde dam our selfes of foly/ as it were to be angry with for-
tune/ that thou canst nat shote an arowe with a plou/ or hunt an
hare with an oxe/ and that some cruell god shulde be agaynst
them/ that with vayn indevour/ hunt an hart with a dragge net/
and nat that they attempt to do those impossibilytes/ by their
own madnesse and folysshnesse. (sig. b. vii^v)

yet now whan none of us sees a vyne beare fygges/ nor an

---

[1] Cf. Horace, *Sermones*, I. 3. 25–7: 'Cum tua pervideas oculis mala lippus
inunctis,/ cur in amicorum vitiis tam cernis acutum/ quam aut aquila aut serpens
Epidaurius?'

[2] *Moralia Plutarchi traducta . . . Plutarchi Liber De Tranquillitate & Securitate
Animi*: G. Budeo (Venice, 1505?).

[3] *Dictionary of Proverbs in England in the 16th and 17th Centuries*, s.v. W603.

olyve beare grapes/ we braule with our selfe neverthelesse.
(sig. c. ii^r)

These two passages, the second of which is clearly a reference to
Luke vi. 44, Wyatt worked up into:

> Non of ye all there is that is so madde
>   To seke grapes upon brambles or breers,
>   Nor none I trow that hath his wit so badd
> To set his hay for Conys over Ryvers,
>   Ne ye set not a dragg net for an hare,
>   And yet the thing that moost is your desire
> Ye do mysseke with more travaill and care.

And this:

for foles let good thynges passe tho they be present/ and regarde
them nat whan they perisshe/ so moche doth their thoughtes
gape gredily after thynges to come. (sig. c. ii^v)

he transformed into a memorable line:

> Madde, if ye list to continue your sore,
>   Let present passe and gape on tyme to come
>   And diepe your self in travaill more and more.

How far can Wyatt's stylistic predilections be linked with the
classical and Renaissance traditions of critical theory on the plain
style which have been so sketchily outlined—or, rather, referred
to—above? What, first of all, are the limitations of an argument
seeking to establish a close relationship between these Humanistic
prescriptions for moral discourses and Wyatt's translation of
The Quyete of Mynde? There are, it seems to me, three reservations
to be made.

Firstly, it would assuredly not be possible to perform for Wyatt
what Trimpi, in the first half of his book, did so thoroughly for
Ben Jonson when he traced a well-defined identity of critical
position (and often of actual language) inextricably linking Jonson

with Seneca, Quintilian, Vives, Lipsius, and Bacon. Not only is
there no commonplace book of literary criticism by Wyatt,
corresponding to the *Discoveries*, which will provide us with
explicit statements about style and clarify his position beyond the
bounds of conjecture, but such a book could not then have been
written. Wyatt stands at the beginning of an English literary
renascence, and there was not behind him, as there was behind
Jonson, an established habit of criticism in and of the vernacular,
a refined critical consciousness evolved from and designed to cope
with an already instituted new literature. Half a century later,
when George Gascoigne presented to *his* queen (also as a New-
Year's gift) a poem which 'even as Petrark in his woorkes *De
remedys utriusque fortunae*, dothe recowmpt the uncerteine Joyes
of men in severall dialogues',[1] that habit was just beginning, and
Wyatt's work was one of its foundations. Furthermore, if Jonson,
in Trimpi's words, was 'one of the great intellectual ambassadors
of the Renaissance',[2] Wyatt was of course a real ambassador and a
busy man. He was not a professional writer, but an amateur, and it
is perhaps significant that his best poems give expression to ideas
and feelings and record experiences that must have arisen directly
out of his professional life as a courtier and a diplomat. The writing
of criticism, even if he had had time and (let us posit, wholly
hypothetically) intellectual inclination for it, would not have
performed the same useful emotional function that we may guess
his poetry did in helping to reconcile him to the changes of
fortune that were so much a part of life at Henry VIII's court. For
these reasons it is inevitable that Wyatt's relation to the theoretical
traditions under discussion should have been relatively unfocused,
unconscious, and inchoate.

Secondly, there would seem to be some contradiction between
what I have claimed was virtually Wyatt's rejection of Petrarch as
out of date and stylistically antipathetic and his manifest accept-
ance of Petrarch as a model (if not as a master) in the love poems.
But this need not give us pause; not all Wyatt's writings, much less

---

[1] *The Grief of Joy* (1577). See *The Steele Glas. etc.: English Reprints*, ed.
Edward Arber (Westminster, 1895), p. 9.
[2] Op. cit., p. 77.

Petrarch's, are of a piece. For the former, the suitability and attractiveness of the plain style as a vehicle for moral discourse would have been perfectly consistent with its obvious inappropriateness to celebrating the delights of the courtly amour or lamenting the pangs of disprized love. As for the Italian, the *De Remediis*—'the most medieval of Petrarch's works'[1]—has little in common with his most original and enduring composition, the *Rime*. Wyatt may willingly have imitated, in the exciting role of pioneer, poetry which treated romantic love more humanly than any since ... Catullus, but the Latin of *De Remediis* offered no new departures.

The third consideration which would seem to weaken the case for seeing Wyatt's prose in terms of the classical plain style and its Renaissance revival is its closeness in many respects to the native English tradition of plain writing. Unadorned colloquiality and the use of homely proverbs were hardly peculiar to the Attic orator; such qualities were central to that unaugmented 'plain and open' style whose development R. W. Chambers traces back to Alfred in *The Continuity of English Prose*.[2] In that essay Chambers says that Thomas More was

> the first Englishman to evolve an effective prose, sufficient for all the purposes of his time: eloquent, dramatic, varied. More can write a prose which is good equally in argument or in narrative, in carefully constructed passages of sustained eloquence, or in rapid dialogue: at times racy and colloquial, at times elaborate...[3]

It could be said of Wyatt with much justice that he achieved such a prose in the Defence, or in the dispatches he sent to Henry from Paris reporting on his audiences with Charles of Spain. It might equally be asserted that Wyatt's successes and failures as a translator in *The Quyete of Mynde* are directly dependent on whether he

---

[1] *Petrarch and His World*, Morris Bishop (Indiana U.P., 1963), p. 330.
[2] This essay forms the Introduction to the *E.E.T.S.* edition of Nicholas Harpsfield's *Life and Death of Sir Thomas More*, 1932.
[3] pp. liii–liv.

aims at the easy native colloquiality of those later productions or is lured into imitating the compact but 'pénible'[1] syntax of Budé's Latin.

This, however, would ignore the formative character of *The Quyete of Mynde* by setting up a false opposition between the English tradition and the classical plain style. Wyatt, cautiously feeling his way in this awkward early effort, often fails, it is true, to capture the natural flow—the 'genius'—of the vernacular. But it was not the insupportableness of the *genus humile* in English that hindered him so much as his inexperience as a translator. If we glance back at Cicero's description of the Attic style we will find nothing that cannot be transplanted with complete natural-ness into English. We may go further still and say that the con-crete, colloquial English and the lucid, unaffected Latin styles reinforce one another by encouraging a synthesis of earthiness and urbanity such as Wyatt was later to achieve in verse in the satires. Trimpi, examining the influence of the *genus humile* on English a century later, observes that:

> Jonson and Bacon, although committed to the doctrine of imitation as everyone in the century was, returned to a classical style, as Vives and others had already done—a style that was, quite by accident perhaps, similar to the English prose that had been in existence long before the 'stylizing' effects of the doc-trine had begun to be apparent.[2]

But the similarity was not accidental. That classical style was attractive for the very reason that it at once sanctioned and supplemented the native: it offered the authority of ancient tradi-tion and neo-Latin scholarship to solid qualities of vigour and homeliness that were already deep-rooted features of English writing, the 'public wealth in a common storehouse' on which Vives lays so much emphasis, while bringing to bear qualities of its own, a range of wit, irony and polished elegance, which alleviated

---

[1] *Guillaume Budé et les Origines de l'Humanisme Français*, Jean Plattard (Paris, 1923), p. 35.
[2] Op. cit., p. 59.

the note of provinciality that had been endemic, particularly in satirical literature, from Langland to Skelton. In Wyatt's most finished works, though not in *The Quyete of Mynde*, the two are choicely blended; to see his role as revolutionary, therefore, would be misguided, for a perception of his place as a Humanist poet at the head of a neo-classical movement which was to continue, sporadically and in much modified forms, for about three hundred years entails no denial of his important and enriching debt to Chaucer. Wyatt's role was both more modest and more useful, for through him we may regard the classical and the native not as conflicting but as complementary traditions.

Despite qualifications, then, it is not fanciful to see in *The Quyete of Mynde*, and still more in Wyatt's expressed attitude to his translation, the germ of this synthesis of classical and English characteristics. And although, as I have said, any connection between Wyatt and Humanist criticism must necessarily be vague and inconclusive and inferred from internal hints, there are, before we leave *The Quyete of Mynde*, a few external circumstances worth adducing in order to illustrate possible points of contact with the cultural milieu that was committed to the 'Senecan' plain style.

Catherine of Aragon, as far as England was concerned with this milieu, occupied a central position. Herself a well-educated woman whose pure Latin and general learning earned Erasmus's admiration (phrased in terms considerably more enthusiastic than any he used of Henry's), she was also an effective patron of Humanist scholarship in England. She tried to keep Erasmus from decamping on his habitual wanderings, and when that proved impossible she tried to lure him back. Catherine was instrumental, too, in drawing her countryman Vives to England, together with his completed manuscript, *De Institutio Christiana Feminae*, which she had commissioned him to write for her—thus following in her mother Queen Isabella's footsteps. Vives, jointly with Thomas Linacre, was tutor to Princess Mary, for whom he prepared a reading list, *De Ratione Studii Puerilis*, where—alongside the pacifist tracts of Erasmus and More's *Utopia*—he recommended Plutarch and Seneca for moral and social guidance. Elsewhere, too, he was to suggest Plutarch for ethical instruction, and in the same breath as Seneca's *De Tranquillitate Animi* and Petrarch's *De Remediis Utriusque Fortunae*.[1] Plutarch's treatises would have been most readily available to Mary in the Latin versions of Erasmus and Guillaume Budé.

It is not without its pathos that Vives later recorded a conversation he had with Catherine in which, discussing the unforeseeable yet ineluctable turns of Fortune's wheel, the Queen—after observing that she had experienced every kind of fortune—declared that she would rather choose a sad lot than the happiest, for there are always consolations to be found in the midst of the great unhappiness, but disproportionate prosperity unhinges one's judgement and piety.[2] Catherine indeed had use for *The Quyete of Mynde*, and she had apparently absorbed its lesson thoroughly.

The third member of the great triumvirate of early sixteenth-century letters, Budé, did not visit England, but pursued his studies at the court of Francis I where he gained a distinguished reputation as the foremost Greek scholar of his time. Like Wyatt he was charged with several diplomatic missions, and it is significant in this context that ambassadors were currently called 'orators'—an expert knowledge of Latin and modern languages being mandatory for any diplomacy more rigorous than the exchange of polite compliments. In 1526, at the start of his career abroad, Wyatt may well have met in Paris the man whose version of Plutarch he was to use the following year. There is no evidence that such a meeting took place, but the opportunity was certainly there and it would be surprising if Wyatt, with his interests and his entrée, failed to make the most of it. At the very least it may be said that, under such powerful Humanist influences, an intellectual atmosphere then pervaded English and French court life that would have encouraged and sustained the production of *The Quyete of Mynde*.

[1] *De Tradendis Disciplinis*, V. 3; ed. cit., p. 252.
[2] See *Opera Omnia*, ed. cit., IV, p. 40.

II

Samuel Daniel's Masque 'The Vision of the Twelve Goddesses'

GEOFFREY CREIGH

DANIEL'S reputation as a deviser of masques, though never high, has progressively diminished in direct proportion to the increasing regard entertained for the masques and entertainments of Ben Jonson. We do not need to look very far for the reason for this; Jonson's cause was that of literary criticism and Daniel's was not. The genesis of the quarrel between Jonson and Daniel, a prologue to the feud conducted so long and so bitterly between Jonson and Inigo Jones, was Jonson's insistence that the masque is a poem while Daniel from the outset contended that the masque is a hybrid form of which poetry constitutes but one element. In recent years a great deal of critical attention has been focussed upon Jonson's aesthetic of the masque and the Jones-Jonson controversy has been fully documented and analysed.[1] Daniel's masques, on the other hand, have been largely neglected or, at best, brought forward even by his apologists as inferior examples of the genre. An examination of Daniel's first masque, *The Vision of the Twelve Goddesses*, reveals a highly developed theory of the nature of masque executed with considerable skill, and the masque itself in no way justifies the critical contempt which has been poured upon it.

Critical debate about the validity of Daniel's method in this masque certainly pre-dates the publication of the first printed authorized edition of the masque in 1604. It is clear from the tone

---

[1] The most comprehensive account of this subject is D. J. Gordon's 'Poet and Architect: The Intellectual Setting of the Quarrel between Ben Jonson and Inigo Jones', *Journal of the Warburg and Courtauld Institutes*, XII (1949), pp. 152–78.

of Daniel's remarks in his preface that an attack upon his practice has already been initiated against which he is concerned to defend himself.[1] This being so, it is unwise to accept his statements in this pamphlet, as they have often been accepted, as detached expressions of theory; Daniel's remarks constitute one side of an argument, and they have a context we can only infer. As Ben Jonson and Inigo Jones repeatedly overreach themselves in their later controversy, Jonson in particular adopting a position so extreme that it in no way reflects the true nature of his collaboration with Jones, so Daniel may here have misrepresented his true position in defending himself against his detractors. The factor of temperament is of relevance also. Whereas both Jones and Jonson were certainly volatile and probably irascible, Daniel was of a diffident and retiring nature, prone to take a depreciatory view of his own work, and generally lacking in self-confidence.[2] A superficial reading of the preface to *The Vision* is misleading for it would appear to suggest that Daniel's view of masque is not far removed from that of Francis Bacon who was later to write of such entertainments that 'these things are but toys to come amongst such serious observations'.[3] It is true that Daniel does write that he conceives the essential function of masque to be 'the decking and furnishing of glory and majesty as the necessary complements requisite for state and greatness',[4] and adds in a statement surely directed

[1] See John C. Meagher, *Method and Meaning in Jonson's Masques* (University of Notre Dame Press, 1966), pp. 14–18.

[2] This fundamental lack of self-confidence is much in evidence in *Musophilus* (1599). The anonymous author of *The Return from Parnassus* also criticizes Daniel on this count.

> Sweet hony dropping *Daniell* may wage
> Warre with the proudest big Italian
> That melts his heart in sugred sonetling:
> Onely let him more sparingly make vse
> Of others wit, and vse his owne the more,
> That well may scorne base imitation.

(*The Three Parnassus Plays (1598–1601)*, ed. J. B. Leishman (London, 1949), pp. 238–9).

[3] Francis Bacon, 'On Masks and Triumphs', *The Essays* etc., ed. Samuel Reynolds (Oxford, 1890), p. 268.

[4] Daniel, *The Vision of the Twelve Goddesses*, ed. Joan Rees in *A Book of Masques*, edd. T. J. Spencer and S. Wells (Cambridge University Press, 1967), p. 25—hereafter cited as *The Vision*.

against Jonson that 'whosoever strives to show most wit about these punctilios of dreams and shows are sure sick of a disease they cannot hide and would fain have the world to think them very deeply learned in all mysteries whatsoever'.[1] Quoted out of context these remarks suggest that Daniel was contemptuous of the form itself, but in their context, that of the total situation, they suggest nothing of the kind. The first statement, neutral in tone, describes the function of the masque without prescribing its nature, whereas the second is personal, angry and hostile, directed by one who no doubt saw himself as a courtier and a scholar against an arrogant and upstart, albeit gifted, bricklayer's son. Daniel's view of Jonson is certainly ungenerous, but as far as we can determine he was not the initiator of the quarrel. To arrive at a legitimate conception of Daniel's view of the nature of masque, it is better to examine his practice as a deviser than to attempt to deduce his theory from a preface apparently provoked by adverse criticism, the precise nature of which we cannot ascertain. Daniel's theory of masque is self-consistent, sophisticated and of a piece with his general aesthetic views; it derives ultimately from his early intellectual commitments and his earliest literary interests.

Among the principal influences in Daniel's intellectual development the work of Sir Philip Sidney has primacy. In later years Daniel was to speak of the time he spent at Wilton House under the patronage of Lady Pembroke, Sidney's sister, as one of the most optimistic and beneficial periods of his life.[2] Sidney's *Defence of Poesie* impressed Daniel and there are a number of points of contact between this work and Daniel's own critical verse essay, *Musophilus*. Like Sidney, Daniel maintains poetry to be the servant of philosophy and as such concerned primarily with truth; and like Sidney, if we may judge from his practice, he conceived of poetry fulfilling this function in Aristotelian terms, by presenting an image of the truth more refined than any that is to be found in the

[1] *The Vision*, p. 30.
[2] Lady Mary Pembroke's patronage of Daniel is discussed by Joan Rees in *Samuel Daniel, A Critical and Biographical Study* (Liverpool University Press, 1964), pp. 43–61.

world of nature. In *The Defence of Poesie* Sidney had written of the
poet that:

> he yeeldeth to the powers of the minde an image of that
> whereof the *Philosopher* bestoweth but a wordish description,
> which doth neither strike, pearce, nor possesse the sight of the
> soule so much, as that other doth.[1]

And further, of the function of poetry itself:

> the final end is, to lead and draw us to as high a perfection, as
> our degenerate soules made worse by their clay-lodgings can be
> capable of.[2]

Sidney's aesthetic is cast in the conventional Aristotelian terms and
he regards poetry as mediating between the ideal reality of the
form and the perceptive faculty capable of apprehending it.
This notion is applied precisely by Daniel both in *The Vision of
the Twelve Goddesses* and in his later masque, *Tethys Festival*,
though in each of these cases the eye as the instrument of the soul
performs an interpretative and mediating function logically prior
but necessarily complementary to that of the understanding.

In a further important respect Daniel remained committed to
his early interests in establishing the foundation for his theory of
the masque. Daniel's masques are highly emblematical and his
earliest publication, probably begun before he left Oxford in
1583, was his translation of Paolo Giovio's treatise on *Imprese* or
emblems, *The Worthy Tract of Paulus Iouius* (1585). To this translation Daniel prefixed a long essay in which he recounts the history
of *Imprese* and also speaks of the rules to be followed in their
composition. The importance of Giovio's treatise to the critic of
the masque is that it is from this work that the terminology subsequently bandied in the Jones–Jonson controversy ultimately
derives. Giovio discusses at length the balance to be maintained

---

[1] *The Prose Works of Sir Philip Sidney*, ed. Albert Feuillerat (Cambridge
University Press, 1963), III, p. 14.
[2] Ibid., p. 11.

between device and motto in the composition of an emblem, stressing that the perfect emblem is characterized by an interpendence of the two parts, which he speaks of as body and soul.

> Knowe you then (Master *Iodouico*) that an inuention or *Impresa* (if it be to be accounted currant) ought to haue these fiue properties, First, iust proportion of body and soule. Secondly, that it be not obscure, that it neede a Sibilla to enterprete it, nor so apparant that euery rusticke may vnderstand it. Thirdly, that it haue especially a beautifull shewe, which makes it become more gallant to the vew, ... Fourthly, that it haue no humane forme. Fifthly, it must haue a posie which is the soule of the body, which ought to differ in language from the *Idioma* of him which beareth the *Impresa*, to the ende the sence may bee the more couert. ... And to make apparant these properties, you shal vnderstand that the body and soule aboue mentioned, is meant either by the mot or by the subiect, and an *Impresa* is accounted vnperfect when the subiect or body beare no proportion of meaning to the soule, or the soule to the body.[1]

That Daniel was profoundly influenced by Giovio's work and that his later support of Inigo Jones in his argument with Jonson is a matter of intellectual rather than personal commitment, is beyond doubt. For Daniel the composition of a masque was an undertaking similar in kind to the composition of an emblem, and the criterion of adequacy was the maintenance of a proper correspondence between the body or visual element and the soul, the poetry. Moreover, for Daniel in *The Vision of the Twelve Goddesses* as for Spenser in *The Masque of Cupid*, for the author of *The Masque of the Adamantine Rock*, and for Jonson in *The Entertainment at Highgate*, and to a lesser extent in *The Masque of Blackness*, the art of making a masque was an emblematical art, and the pleasure to be taken by the spectator in experiencing and interpreting the action was of the same kind as he would experience in reading an *Impresa*. Daniel, more consistent though in-

[1] S. Daniel, *The Worthy Tract of Paulus Iouius* etc. (London, 1585), Biii^v–Biiii.

finitely less flexible than Jonson in his conception of the form, is deeply rooted in the emblematical tradition, and in neither of his masques does he permit, as Jonson increasingly does, the claim of dramatic poetry to disturb what he conceives to be the necessary balance between the visual and the poetic. The pleasure the spectator enjoys, as in the reading of *Imprese*, is the pleasure of recognition. The understanding meditates upon those images which enter at the eye and is assisted by the measure of prose or verse illumination judged appropriate to the occasion. The universal nature of such pleasure is described at length by Daniel in his preface to *The Worthy Tract of Paulus Iouius*:

> Yet I say, that to represent vnto the sence of sight the forme or figure of any thing is more natural in act, and more common to al creatures then is hearing, and thereupon sayth Aristotle, that we loue the sence of seeing, for that by it we are taught and made to learne more then by any other of our sences, whereby we see that all men naturally take delight in pictures . . . in which facultie the Aegyptians were most singulare as the first authors of this *Hieroglyphicall* art: as well do witnesse their sacred Colomnes dedicated to *Mercurie*, whereon were diuers formes and pictures wrought and engrauen, contayning great knowledge, which they called *Hieroglyphi*. To which pillers Plato is sayde to haue gone and retourned with great profit. Yet notwithstanding, in my opinion their deuise was vnperfect, by reason of the diuersitie of the natures of beastes and other things which they figured. Whereupon they who drewe more neere vnto our time seemeth to haue brought this art to perfection, by adding mots or posies to their figures whereby they couertly disclose their intent by a more perfect order. Moreouer besides the figuring of things corporall and of visible forme, men haue also represented things incorporal. . . .[1]

Clearly then, when in 1610, in his preface to *Tethys Festival*, Daniel makes his one substantial contribution to the Jones–Jonson controversy and forcibly argues the dependence of poet upon architect in the devising of masques, it is not simply because he is

[1] Ibid., Ai^v–Aii.

c

'at Jealousies'[1] with Jonson, nor can his comments be dismissed as 'testy and pedestrian'.[2] It can be demonstrated that *The Vision of the Twelve Goddesses* reveals that as early as 1603 Daniel had conceived a theory of masque which was both intellectually respectable and dramatically viable; that he comprehended as fully as anyone the nature of the occasion on which the masque at Court was conventionally performed, and that he succeeded in providing the Court with an entertainment entirely appropriate to this occasion.

Critics of the masque have been severe with Daniel's first attempt in this genre and are more or less united in their dismissal of *The Vision* as a monument to dead ideas, a cumbersome emblematic procession amounting, in Orgel's view, to 'little more than pageantry' and lacking 'dramatic coherence'.[3] Herford and Simpson considered the piece 'structureless and old-fashioned'.[4] The masque is also ridiculed by Brotanek[5] while Professor G. Bentley finds that Daniel fails to 'reveal the faintest hint of Jonson's high conception of the form and function of the masque'.[6] Notwithstanding its current reputation, however, there is no doubt that Daniel's masque was well received by the Court and that it occasioned a great deal of contemporary interest. It appears to have been the first entertainment of its kind to have been independently printed, appearing in two editions, one authorized and the other surreptitious. A letter written by Dudley Carleton to his friend John Chamberlain testifies to the enthusiastic manner in which the entertainment was received at the Court.[7]

Daniel's sense of the nature of the occasion of which the masque is the centre piece controls his conception of the form. It is clear that he thinks of the masque as a form in which the spectators

---

[1] Ben Jonson, *The Works*, edd. Herford and Simpson (Oxford, 1925), I, p. 136.

[2] As Professor Bentley does in *A Book of Masques*, op. cit., p. 4.

[3] Stephen Orgel, *The Jonsonian Masque* (Harvard University Press, 1965), p. 101.

[4] Ben Jonson, *The Works*, X, p. 450.

[5] Rudolph Brotanek, *Die Englischen Maskenspiele* (Vienna and Leipzig, 1902), pp. 130–1.

[6] Op. cit., p. 4.

[7] *S.P.D.* I, VI, 21. Reprinted by E. K. Chambers in *The Elizabethan Stage* (Oxford, 1923), III, pp. 279–80.

participate, although their participation is mute. In *The Vision of the Twelve Goddesses* Daniel's principal concern is to provide the Court with the opportunity of celebrating its own proper identity; the dramatic centre piece, the masque itself, achieves its full significance only in terms of its successful interrelation with its specific context. In *The Vision of the Twelve Goddesses* Daniel sets out to represent to James, to the foreign ambassadors and the spectators at large, an idealized image of the English Court tactfully implying at the same time that with the accession of James the ideal and the real have become, or at least should have become, identified.

The Vision is essentially processional and emblematical in structure and the written speeches and songs are economical and interrelated with the total design. Though far from structureless, the scenario of the masque is simple. Daniel makes use of a dispersed setting having at one end of the Great Hall a mountain from which the goddesses descend in triadic procession and at the further end a Temple of Virtue and the Cave of Somnus. The plot is straightforward. Night awakes her son, Sleep, from his cave. Sleep carries two wands, one white to evoke meaningful and instructive visions and one black to promote confused dreams. The spectators are initiated into the ritual to follow when Sleep flourishes his white wand and retires to his cave. The dramatic action then begins. First Iris, the messenger of the goddesses, proceeds from the mountain to the temple to warn the Sibilla in attendance there of the approach of the goddesses, presenting her with a 'prospective' or telescope through which she may view them before they descend. This device serves the practical end of removing the necessity of interrupting the flow of the later action, for the Sibilla proceeds to identify the goddesses and to describe them prior to their descent into the Court. The goddesses then proceed in threes (each rank interspersed with a triad of torchbearers) from the mountain to the temple bearing emblems designating the particular virtues they are to be taken to represent, and these are deposited on the altar.[1] Whilst this procession is in

[1] *Juno* (Power) carries a sceptre; *Pallas* (Wisdom and Defence) a lance and target; *Venus* (Love and Amity) a scarf; *Vesta* (Religion) a burning lamp;

progress the three Graces further point its significance with their accompanying song. The Measures follow, after which the Graces sing once again before the masquers select their partners from the audience and dance with them. A short retiring dance performed by the masquers precedes their return to the mountain and thus the entertainment ends.

The basic simplicity of Daniel's design is admirable and it conceals a purpose which is both serious and sophisticated. Daniel's expressed intention in the masque was to 'present the figure of those blessings, with the wish of their increase and continuance, which this mighty kingdom now enjoys by the benefit of his most gracious Majesty, by whom we have this glory of peace',[1] a theme closely related to that of the *Panegyrike Congratulatorie* with which he had greeted James at Burley-on-the-Hill the previous year. For Daniel mere pageantry will not suffice. He clearly sees the occasion, that of James's first Christmas in London, as one of great political significance, and his consciousness of the nature of the occasion is reflected in the total design of the masque.

Daniel's first concern is to establish the ground upon which the masque is to be entertained, and it is to this end that the prospective or telescope is introduced.[2] Somnus has already initiated the spectators into a mystery, and the telescope, the essential property of which is to distort vision by providing a point of view other than the natural, enables the Sibilla to proceed beyond the natural and to perceive a higher reality than that which is to be apprehended by the human eye. The goddesses discerned by the Sibilla on the mountain are revealed to her as the virtues they traditionally represent. It was therefore beside the point to object to Daniel's

[1] *The Vision*, p. 25.

[2] It serves of course, as Daniel states, the further practical end of obviating the necessity of interrupting the subsequent action when 'pomp and splendour of the sight takes up all the intention without regard what is spoken' (*The Vision*, p. 29).

Diana (Chastity) a bow and quiver; *Proserpina* (Riches) golden ore; *Macaria* (Felicity) a cadaceum; *Concordia* (Union of Hearts) a branch of intertwined roses; *Astraea* (Justice) a sword and balance; *Flora* (Earth) Flowers; *Ceres* (Plenty) a sickle; and *Tethes* (Power by sea) a trident.

practice on the grounds that his figures were not 'drawn in all proportions to the life of antiquity'.[1] Myth and history are not to be confused. When the goddesses descend from their mountain, they do so as:

> figures wherein antiquity hath formerly clothed them and as they have been cast in the imagination of piety, who hath given mortal shapes to the gifts and effects of an eternal power, for that those beautiful characters of sense were easier to be read, than their mystical *Ideas*, dispersed in that wide and incomprehensible volume of nature.[2]

Daniel's manipulation of the nature of reality is deliberate and it enables him to pay an effective compliment to the Queen and the other ladies personating the goddesses. That they incarnate virtue, he suggests, is no more a fiction than to suppose that virtue was ever incarnate. The ladies of James's Court thus not only represent the goddesses; they are seen to be as real as the goddesses they represent. They embody those virtues they confer upon the Court into which they now formally descend. The use of the prospective glass is further justified in the conceit that their physical presence is so resplendent that it will 'bereave (the spectators) of all save admiration and amazement, for who can look upon such Powers and speak?'[3] Their beauty dazzles the beholders but their correlative virtue has been defined and expressed by the Sibilla who discerns not only the outward show, but beyond this the true essences of things. The total conceit is entirely Platonic.[4]

[1] That Daniel was so accused, possibly by Jonson, is clear from his comments prefaced to *Tethys Festival* (1610). 'And for these figures of mine, if they come not drawn in all proportions to the life of antiquity (from whose tyranny I see no reason why we may not emancipate our inventions) yet I know them such as were proper to the business . . .' (*Works*, ed. Grosart, III, p. 307).

[2] *The Vision*, p. 32.

[3] Ibid., p. 32.

[4] The parable of the Cave is probably relevant. The eye of the 'prisoner', accustomed to the world of shadows, is dazzled by excess of brightness when the prisoner is led out of his cave and confronted by a higher reality. (*The Republic*, VII, 514-18.)

The progress of the goddesses from the mountain at the lower end of the Hall to the temple at the upper end is accompanied by the first of two songs sung by a chorus of three Graces. The song encapsulates much of the topical political significance of the entertainment and is entirely appropriate to the occasion. Daniel is drawing upon a rich tradition in presenting these figures, and his treatment of the Graces—not the conventional figures of the neoplatonic triad, *Pulchitrudo, Amor* and *Voluptus*—is nevertheless sanctioned by classical authority. For Daniel, as for the Florentine Neoplatonists, the ultimate source of information on the signification of this complex icon is Seneca; and in presenting the triad 'Desert, Reward and Gratitude', Daniel is following closely Seneca's account of Chrysippus's interpretation of the image. The relevant passage occurs in Seneca's *De Beneficiis*:

> . . . quare tres Gratiae et quare sorores sint, et quare manibus inplexis, et quare ridentes et iuuenes et uirgines solutaque ac perlucida ueste. Alii quidem uideri uolunt unam esse, quae det beneficium, alteram, quae accipiat, tertiam, quae reddat; alii tria beneficorum esse genera promerentium, reddentium, simul accipientium reddentiumque. Sed utrumlibet ex istis iudica verum: quid ista nos scientia iuuat? Quid ille consertis manibus in se redeuntium chorus? Ob hoc, quia ordo beneficii per manus transeuntis nihilo minus ad dantem reuertitur et totius speciem perdit, si usquam interruptus est, pulcherrimus, si cohaeret interim et uices seruat. In eo est aliqua tamen maioris dignatio sicut promerentium.[1]

Golding's translation of 1578 renders the passage as follows:

> . . . why there bee three Graces, why they bee sisters, and why they go hand in hand: why they looke smyling, why they bee yoong, and why they bee maidens, and appareled in looce and sheare raiment. Some would have it ment thereby, that one of them bestoweth the good turne [,] the other receiveth it, and the thirde requiteth it. Othersome meene that there bee three sortes of benefyting: that is too wit, of befreendyng, of requyting, and both of receiuyng and requyting together. But take whiche

---

[1] Seneca, *De Beneficiis* I, III, 2–4.

of these you list to bee trew. What dooth this maner of knowledge profite vs? Why walkes that knot in a roundell hand in
hand? It is in this respect, that a good turne passing orderly from
hand to hand, dooth neuerthelesse returne too the giuer: and the
grace of the whole is mard, if it bee anywhere broken of: but
is most beautifull, if it continew toogether and keepe his course.[1]

Daniel's presentation of the Graces follows Seneca's account and
elaborates upon it. As Ficino had seen in the configuration of the
Graces the circle of divine love, the ultimate image of cosmic
harmony,[2] so Daniel turns the moral towards the Court, and
presents the Graces in a social context in which they are seen as
mirroring the circle of divine love in terms appropriate to society
at large and the Court, the superior microcosm of that society, in
particular:

> Desert, Reward and Gratitude,
> The Graces of society,
> Do here with hand in hand conclude
> The blessed chain of amity:
> For we deserve, we give, we thank,
> Thanks, gifts, deserts, thus join in rank.
>
> We yield the splendent rays of light,
> Unto these blessings that descend:
> The grace whereof with more delight
> The well disposing doth commend;
> Whilst Gratitude, Rewards, Deserts,
> Please, win, draw on, and couple hearts.
>
> For worth and power and due respect,
> Deserves, bestows, returns with grace
> The meed, reward, the kind effect
> That give the world a cheerful face,
> And turning in this course of right,
> Make virtue move with true delight.[3]

[1] Arthur Golding, *The Woorke of the excellent Philosopher Lucius Annaeus Seneca concerning Benefyting, that is too say the dooing, receyuing, and requyting of good Turnes* (London, 1578), A iii–A iii^v.
[2] For a full account of the treatments of this image in Renaissance iconology, see Edgar Wind, *Pagan Mysteries in the Renaissance* (London, 1958), pp. 31–56.
[3] *The Vision*, p. 35.

The Graces song is entirely appropriate to the action which it accompanies. As the goddesses lay emblems of the particular virtues they represent upon the altar of the temple, the Graces define the nature of the moral climate in which these gifts can most effectively flourish.

The emblematical gifts having been deposited upon the altar, the dancers perform their measures 'with great majesty and art, consisting of divers strains, framed unto motions circular, square, triangular, with other proportions exceeding rare and full of variety'.[1] It is likely that the choreography was integral to the total concept of the masque, but unfortunately we possess no record of its precise nature. The measures, however, certainly symbolized in the traditional manner concord and harmony, thus celebrating the ideal nature of society which is to move in imitation of the greater cosmic harmony. The measures completed, the Graces again sing while the ladies symbolically initiate the Court at large into their own assumed higher reality as they select their partners from amongst the spectators and perform a further set of dances with them. Having thus once more symbolically conferred their favours or blessings upon the Court, they perform a final measure before Iris announces their departure and they reascend the mountain in the same order as that which marked their descent.

Iris's final speech sustains the underlying Platonic theme of the masque and provides further evidence of Daniel's self-conscious manipulation of overlapping layers of reality, so important an aspect of the world of masque. Daniel remains faithful to his earlier delimitation of the validity of myth and skilfully turns it to artistic advantage. As the goddesses of antiquity were themselves human representations of divine powers, 'characters of sense . . . easier to be read than their mystical *Ideas*',[2] so do these Powers, represented by former times 'in the shape and name of women'[3] now discover in the Queen and the ladies of her Court 'the best (and most worthily the best) of ladies . . . whose forms they presently

---

[1] Ibid., p. 30.
[2] Ibid., p. 31.
[3] Ibid., pp. 25–6.

undertook as delighting to be in the best-built temples of beauty and honour'.[1] It is not enough that the Court of James has been shown to be comparable to Olympus; ultimately it has been shown to belong to a higher order of reality and is therefore to be preferred before it.

It is not really necessary, as has become fashionable, to decry Daniel in order to pay Jonson his proper due. The sophistication and quality of Daniel's mind are evident in his conception of this masque and here, as in *Tethys Festival*, his honesty and fair-mindedness are revealed in his generous allowance of the claims of poet, choreographer and architect; and with characteristic modesty he did not exaggerate the claims of the poet. As a poet Daniel is not Jonson's inferior though he lacks Jonson's flexibility and dramatic skill. As an entertainment, however, *The Vision of the Twelve Goddesses* has its own unique merit, blending didacticism, spectacle and poetry in a pleasing and intelligent manner. It warrants greater respect than it has been paid.

[1] Ibid., pp. 36–7.

III

Bedlam and Parnassus: Eighteenth-Century Reflections

SANDY CUNNINGHAM

So readily does our criticism wax moralistic, so keen to sound improving, and so (rightly) eager have we been to reclaim the Augustans from disparagement, that it almost ceases to cause surprise to hear them spoken of, especially Pope and Swift, as if there were no significant limitations and little to cause lasting perplexity in the posture they adopt towards their own time and towards the nature of man. Discussion of them tends to move from an exposition of their general convictions, social, ethical, political, metaphysical, into the detailed interpretation of their work, seen as exhibiting a play of wit and intelligence consistent with this firm established base. *An Essay on Man* becomes the profound philosophical companion to *The Dunciad*, cognate expressions of the one Enlightenment. Swift's wit, explicable at last, relinquishes peculiarities and terrors: we may dare to *agree* with him! When yet another school anthology declares, by way of simply adequate description, that Pope is a 'neoclassic', one wants to say not simply that the term sits better on a dunce, but also that some of the deficiencies Pope visits upon his dunces reflect on the quality and scope of his own recourse to classical humanist tradition. Olympus and Bedlam, Grub Street and Parnassus, reason and folly, heroes and fops: the antitheses decidedly polarize our attention; but they quickly forsake their stable state, become equivocal, yield paradox, merge and recede, look rather more like tautologies than opposites—Grub Street thronged with Parnassians, reason the high *priori* road to folly, the ponderous also ephemeral, Olympus an antique drum. The stable state is often less exciting than the volatile, and we need not constantly try to rationalize wit's accomplishments in terms of a system of values we can convey in an expository fashion. Besides, wit may sometimes not only expose the dull, but mask the wit's own dullness.

To wish away some of our persistent *justifying* of the Augustans need not lead us, on the other hand, to revive the predilections of dilute Romantic criticism. The tradition that diagnosed the limitations of eighteenth-century poetry as those inevitably attendant on an 'Age of Reason' led eventually to A. E. Housman's absurd dismissive aphorisms: 'Meaning is of the intellect, poetry is not. If it were, the eighteenth century would have been able to write it better.'[1] The poets of genuine talent, he argued, invoking Plato and the fine frenzy, transcended their age because they were mad: four mad men, the century's true poets, Collins, Cowper, Smart, and ... Blake. In the same context, Housman identified poetry, with a display of diffidence, as 'a secretion; whether a natural secretion, like turpentine in the fir, or a morbid secretion, like the pearl in the oyster. I think that my own case, though I may not deal with the material so cleverly as the oyster does, is the latter'.[2] Housman might not have been dismayed to find that his emphasis on the frenzied and the involuntary ranged him with the possessed bards of *The Dunciad*, whose relatives are the innumerable fixated inmates of Augustan satire. But he might have wanted to disown a much more exact ancestor, the upside-down Longinus-Horace of *The Art of Sinking in Poetry*, who offers it as 'an undoubted physical maxim, that poetry is a *natural or morbid secretion from the brain*':

> As I would not suddenly stop a cold in the head or dry up a neighbour's issue, I would as little hinder him from necessary writing. It may be affirmed with great truth that there is hardly any human creature past childhood but at one time or other has had some poetical evacuation, and no question was much the better for it in his health; so true is the saying, 'we are born poets'. Therefore is the desire of writing properly termed *pruritus*, the *titillation of the generative faculty of the brain*; and the person is said to conceive (Chapter 3).

[1] *The Name and Nature of Poetry* (1933), pp. 38–9.
[2] Ibid., pp. 48–9.

This is, of course, one of many ventriloquist dolls who cite
Augustan scripture to plausible but ridiculous effect. He confounds
the erotic and the cloacal in true duncely mode, and zealously
avails himself of an important truth from Horace in a context
that deforms it. His athletic contemporaries dive into the sewers of
The Dunciad. The more puzzling voice of Swift's *Mechanical
Operation of the Spirit* insists that all human pretensions to vision or
disinterested speculative thought or idealism are equally the pro-
ducts of libidinous zeal, ridiculously unacknowledged. Such a
levelling spirit, in both witty forms and plain, can often be met
with among the Augustans. Eighteenth-century literature fills
Bedlam and Grub Street to overflowing; but a mirror held up to
fools and dunces is also inescapably a mirror to the creator of the
dunce. If there is a Parnassian in the fool, and a reasoner in the
madman, there may be more of a dunce in the Augustan than he is
always ready or able to recognize. That would not be to catch him
out: witty creativity sharpens the criteria by which in its turn it is
judged.

As an institution, given over to the confinement of lunatics,
Bethlehem Hospital, or Bedlam, was an infant compared with its
rival, the abode of true inspiration, Parnassus. Henry VIII had
handed over the suppressed convent as a place to house the mad as
recently as 1547. Confining Tom o' Bedlam had, of course, perhaps still has, the deepest consequences for the rational and
orderly citizen whose soul was not possessed, whether of angels or
the devil. It institutionalized the sane man's conviction that he is a
totally different kind of creature, though an actual encounter with
a madman might prove him to be tractable, even civil. Thomas
Hobbes's discussion of madness, 'whereof there be almost as many
kinds, as of the Passions themselves', leads him to consider, among
other lunatics, those 'that are possessed of an opinion of being
inspired'. This particular madness need not, he argues, be exhi-
bited in violent activity for it to be recognized as insanity: 'that
very arrogating such inspiration to themselves, is argument
enough'. Hobbes goes on, with urbane dry wit, to illustrate the
point from an imagined Sunday tour of Bedlam, that recreation so
dear to the polite, one that forms a kind of model for much of

the satiric writing of the Augustans. Hobbes presents us with this case:

> If some man in Bedlam should entertaine you with sober discourse; and you desire in taking leave, to know what he were, that you might another time requite his civility; and he should tell you, he were God the Father; I think you need expect no extravagant action for argument of his Madnesse.[1]

This polite conversation, a discourse of reason between madman and sane in which each of them is delightfully proficient, does not encourage Hobbes to give the Bedlamite's claim to divinity even a sceptical consideration. We might reasonably regret that this promising sabbatical relationship is assumed properly to end here, at this point of definitive diagnosis. But there was much to persuade the mid-century, a dozen years before *Paradise Lost*, that the madman's conviction about his identity would prove incurable, however incorrect.

Let us suppose the visitor in Hobbes's story to be Pope, some eighty years later, intent on requiting God's civility by vindicating his extravagant action to post-Restoration man, man 'united in the bounds of a rational society'. Had the Bedlamite produced passages from the work of Pope or Swift that could be construed as demolishing all hope of rational and honest public conduct and government, Pope might have responded by offering him a consolation of philosophy from *An Essay on Man*. The madman's case, he might have said, was quite normal—indeed, providentially so: we all survive as contented creatures *because* we are creatures of folly, well deceived, inheritors of what Hobbes himself called 'the privilege of absurdity'. Each of us, naturally proficient, swims with bladders of philosophy or fantasy towards each new horizon, or is content with the old, ridiculously self-engrossed, risibly hopeful:

> The learn'd is happy nature to explore,
> The fool is happy that he knows no more;
> The rich is happy in the plenty giv'n,
> The poor contents him with the care of Heav'n.

[1] *Leviathan* (1651); ed. C. B. Macpherson (Pelican Books, 1968), p. 141.

> See the blind beggar dance, the cripple sing.
> The sot a hero, lunatic a king;
> The starving chemist in his golden views
> Supremely blest, the poet in his muse.[1]

It is a passage of astounding despatch and confidence, given the scope of its anatomy of human contentment: *King Lear* and *Don Quixote* are among the works that give authority, however distantly, to these suave couplets. Supremely blest in trenchant generalization, does the author of these lines implicitly exempt himself from the diagnosis?

If our attention is drawn from this passage into other works of Pope, we may light on the opening of *The Dunciad*, Book III, written rather earlier. Delusions of grandeur are here presented not as one feature of our native state of folly, but as symptoms of depravity, the flight from rationality:

> Then raptures high the seat of Sense o'erflow,
> Which only heads refin'd from Reason know.
> Hence, from the straw where Bedlam's Prophet nods,
> He hears loud Oracles, and talks with Gods:
> Hence the Fool's Paradise, the Statesman's Scheme,
> The air-built Castle, and the golden Dream,
> The Maid's romantic wish, the Chemist's flame,
> And Poet's vision of eternal Fame.[2]

Blind self-delusion, Utopian dream, religious vision: in one set of terms these constitute our normal, necessary foolishness; in the other, they are the peculiar province of abandoned sense. The line between the two accounts is fine; but the two passages afford an example of a competition frequently met with in Augustan writing. It is that between a mockery so comprehensive that it should include the mockery itself, and the isolation of some behaviour as an aberration from the norm. We are all mad, whether in using reason or abandoning it; alternatively, those of us are mad who give up reason and sense. The competing views are often hard to

[1] Epistle II, ll. 263–70.
[2] Book III, ll. 5–12.

separate; that they are often both present is of major importance to the kinetic vigour, and the complexity, of the Augustan response to human behaviour.

Pope's insistence in places on Folly as a sustaining normal human characteristic owes a good deal, of course, to Erasmus's *Praise of Folly*. His dependence on Erasmus's mischievous delight in exploding our assumption that our best source of wisdom and consolation is the wakeful, reasoning mind is shared most notably by a self-confessed madman impersonated by Swift. The mad reasoner of the 'Digression Concerning Madness' in *A Tale of a Tub* had been delighted by a typically spirited piece of Erasmian subversion:

> And what can be more faunyng, than whan one man praiseth an other? *lyke moles clawyng eche others backe*? Or what nedeth me to allege vnto you, how this flaterie supplieth a great good porcion of that famous *Eloquence*, greatter percell of *Phisike*, and greatest of *Poetrie*? at ones, that she is euin the verie hony, and conserue of mans societee and companiyng togethers?

> But *Philosophers* saie it is a *miserable thyng to be begyled, and erre so*. Naie, most miserable is it (I saie) not to erre, and not to be deceiued. For too too are thei deceiued, who wene that mans felicitee consisteth in things selfe, and not rather in the opinion how the same are taken. *In as muche as in all humaine thynges, there is so great darkenesse and diuersnesse, as nothyng maie be clerely knowne out, nor discouered*: lyke as truely was affirmed by my *Academicall philosophers*, the lest arrogant amonges all theyr *Sectes*. Or if that ought maie be knowen, the same yet not seldome disauaileth to the gladsomenesse and pleasure of the lyfe. Lastly, so is mans mynde framed, as muche more it deliteth in thynges to the shew, than in suche as are in deede.[1]

Another element in Erasmus, supplemented by Montaigne, confirms Pope's rational scepticism about the accomplishments of rationality:

> On human actions reason tho' you can,
> It may be reason, but it is not man.[2]

[1] *The Praise of Folie*, trans. Chaloner (1549); ed. C. H. Miller (Oxford (E.E.T.S.), 1965), p. 63.
[2] *Moral Essays*, Epistle I, ll. 35–6.

Swift's mad reasoner presses both scepticism and the gospel of Folly to the service of a nonsense argument that is uncomfortably close to the received discourse of reason, and shot through with persuasive insights and hints of the author's own convictions. This is, we remind ourselves, Swift's mimicry of a dunce's mimicry of an Augustan. If Reason does no more, in its dull anatomizing of experience, than offer us truisms about the gap between appearance and reality, and about how despicable and innately foolish we are, and if we have a natural predilection for concealment and a distaste for the truth, then we do well to renounce inquiry altogether, says the madman, and embrace whole-heartedly any philosophy that will justify our being willingly deluded. With a kind of foggy coherence, the argument rationalizes the force of such a line as 'the sot a hero, lunatic a king' by leading to a proposal that the Bedlamites should be released, as they are models of what passes among ourselves for sanity. 'What wonderful talents are here displayed!' In terms that Pope could have used to cheer up Hobbes's madman—if thinking you are God the Father makes you happy, why choose truth?

We are being lured into identifying Swift's mad reasoner as the author of Pope's consolatory passage. To do so would be to qualify as one of those who, in Dr. Johnson's austere phrase, 'being able to add nothing to truth, hope for eminence from the heresies of paradox'.[1] But the blithe reductiveness of the one seems to reveal deficiencies in the witty moralizing of the other. And if we pursue analysis of the madman's argument in such a way as to exonerate *Swift* from all concurrence with his speaker's attitudes, with their undesirable qualities, we are expurgating it, and diminishing its power to puzzle us.

If we turn to Johnson while on this theme, we find him providing on the one hand biting criticism of Pope's cheering wisdom, and on the other his own variant of the deliberate abandonment of rational inquiry in the interest of attaining quietude. The criticism occurs in the famous review of Soame Jenyns's *Enquiry*:

This author and Pope perhaps never saw the miseries which

[1] Preface to Shakespeare, *Yale Edition of Johnson*, Vol. VII, p. 59.

they imagine thus easy to be borne . . . I never yet knew disorders of the mind increase felicity.[1]

In *Rasselas*, Imlac begins his account of madness, 'The Dangerous Prevalence of Imagination', with a sober version of the insistence that the sane are all, to some degree, not sane: 'Perhaps, if we speak with rigorous exactness, no human mind is in its right state.' The sentence has a power to disconcert us rivalled only rarely—perhaps, as one contender, by Montaigne's 'The worst place we can take is in our selves', an observation Johnson himself would have understood only too well.[2] Montaigne displays a curious genial composure in the face of extremes of scepticism and 'the heresies of paradox': undismayed by the assertion that it is through sleep and madness that we attain all the wisdom worth attaining. Johnson, by contrast, can be brought to pray in anguish for release from the ramifying complications produced by sceptical rationalism—'unprofitable and dangerous inquiries . . . difficulties vainly curious . . . doubts impossible to be solved'.[3] But it is equally Johnson who can assert, through Imlac, and from equal inwardness with despair, that the use of reason is to keep madness at bay:

All power of fancy over reason is a degree of insanity; but while this power is such as we can controul and repress, it is not visible to others, nor considered as any deprivation of the mental faculties: it is not pronounced madness but when it becomes ungovernable, and apparently influences speech or action.

To indulge the power of fiction, and send imagination out upon the wing, is often the sport of those who delight too much in silent speculation. When we are alone we are not always busy; the labour of excogitation is too violent to last long; the ardour of inquiry will sometimes give way to idleness and satiety. He who has nothing external to divert him, must find pleasure in his own thoughts, and must fancy himself what he is not; for who is pleased with what he is?

[1] Johnson, *Works* (1806), Vol. VIII, pp. 31–2.
[2] Montaigne, 'An Apologie of Raymond Sebond', trans. Florio; in *Essayes*, ed. Seccombe (Grant Richards, 1908), Vol II, p. 350.
[3] A diary entry of 12 August, 1784. *Yale Edition of Johnson*, Vol. I, pp. 383–4.

D

In time some particular train of ideas fixes the attention, all other intellectual gratifications are rejected, the mind, in weariness or leisure, recurs constantly to the favourite conception, and feasts on the luscious falsehood whenever she is offended with the bitterness of truth. By degrees the reign of fancy is confirmed; she grows first imperious, and in time despotick. Then fictions begin to operate as realities, false opinions fasten upon the mind, and life passes in dreams of rapture or of anguish.[1]

The ingredients are familiar: reason and the actual aligned in opposition to fancy and the seductively fictitious; our real condition something we must either be diverted from considering, or displace with an ideal we will not attain. But reliance on the received antitheses characterizes Johnson's thinking here in no arbitrary, convenient way. It carries the tenor of a rigorous, even a heroic, vigilance over a delinquent selfhood. Nothing could be further from the glib recourse of Swift's mad reasoner to just the same antitheses, weaving an argument in justification of those appetites Johnson feels to be naturally, but reprehensibly, strong. But we may agree that Johnson is also in his own way a victim of the limitations of his terms. In their most intractable form, denied the blurred edges of self-directed irony, or the specious complications of paradox, the Augustan opposites seem all too likely to induce despair. Slightly off-guard, as he will often be, the rational Augustan finds himself in Bedlam among the madmen who are talking variants of his own idiom. Costly, the torments reason helps induce and cannot long allay.

The Vanity of Human Wishes calls for silence on another powerful Augustan theme: we are characterized, indeed caricatured, by one fixated aspiration or another, each of them definable by what it cannot attain—conquest by invincibility, long life by immortality, love by respect. In the context of *An Essay on Man*, such a conviction would be alleviated by the dexterous behaviour of its tone, by the suggestion of command, and by the competition of numerous other convictions offered as also at least partly true. Even so, there is something all too con-

[1] *Rasselas*, ch. xliv.

venient about Pope's Ruling Passion theory: one might have a
ruling passion for analysing people's ruling passions! In Johnson's
poem, the sole retreat from the self-inflicted defeats of the
fixated lies quite outside the zone of rational appraisals of experience. An active pious resignation is offered as the last resort, a
self-administered anaesthetic. If it is too painfully true for Johnson
to assure Hobbes's madman he is normal, it remains to encourage
him to pray, in the hope of his becoming relatively happy in
another way that is nevertheless, like his conviction of divinity,
sadly unsupported by the facts:

> These goods for man the laws of heav'n ordain,
> The goods he grants, who grants the pow'r to gain;
> With these celestial wisdom calms the mind,
> And makes the happiness she does not find. (ll. 365–8)

Not the serenity of a fool among knaves, but something that may
look quite like it, that of a saint among fools. We may well feel
that this offered solace is vulnerable in its turn to the poem's own
despairing insistence on the futility of wishing. If so, it contributes
to the conclusion's tragic dignity.

At the gates of Bedlam, the statues of Raving Madness and
Melancholy Madness, 'Great Cibber's brazen brainless brothers',
presided recumbently over the madhouse itself and the adjacent
'Cave of Poverty and Poetry'. Pope remarks, in a footnote, 'how
near allied Dulness is to Madness'.[1] Augustan satire gifts besotted
contentment with a dynamism, pedantry with vivacious zeal,
bathos with raptures of its own. The dull poet, tone-deaf, is
paradoxically exalted into a frenzy of nonsense with ingredients of
discrimination and sense. His ponderous art of sinking produces,
consistent with the surprising ballistics of lead, astounding ascents
into a heaven of absurd invention—'forc'd from wind-guns, lead
itself can fly':

> What crouds of these, impenitently bold,
> In Sounds and jingling Syllables grown old,

[1] *The Dunciad* (1743), Book I, l. 33 n.

Still run on Poets in a raging vein,
Ev'n to the dregs and squeezings of the brain:
Strain out the last, dull droppings of their sense,
And rhyme with all the rage of impotence![1]

As masters of heavy levitation, they are the successors of Rochester's pedantic visionaries whose nonsense discourse interpreting the mysteries of Creation is conducted in 'those Reverend *Bedlams, Colledges,* and *Schools*'.[2] If, as Pope's imagery insists, creative effort (the Use of Literacy) becomes both widespread and abdominal, a sanitary problem arises. In Dublin, a public-spirited Swiftian urges the provision of metaphysical sewers to meet the crisis:

> I believe our corrupted *Air*, and frequent thick *Fogs* are in a great measure owing to the common exposal of our *Wit*, and that with good Management, our Poetical *Vapours* might be carried off in a *common Drain*, and fall into one Quarter of the Town, without infecting the whole, as the Case is at present, to the great Offence of our *Nobility*, our *Gentry*, and *Others* of nice *Noses*.[3]

He suggests the confinement of mad creators, on the model of Grub Street:

> some *private Street*, or *blind Alley* of this Town may be fitted up at the charge of the Publick, as an Apartment for the *Muses*, (like those at *Rome*, and *Amsterdam*, for their Female Relations) and be wholly consign'd to the uses of our *WITS*.

Dunce after dunce, in Pope and Swift, argues for solidarity and trade-union recognition, premature Tolpuddle martyrs for a pantomime Equity. They seek the corporate blessing for each one to satisfy his private predilections, each entitled to a cell in the

[1] Pope, *An Essay on Criticism*, ll. 604–9. The wind-guns are found in *The Dunciad*, Book I, l. 181.

[2] 'A Satyr against Mankind', l. 83. *Poems*, ed. V. de Sola Pinto (Routledge, 1953), p. 120.

[3] Swift, *A Letter of Advice to a Young Poet*; in *Irish Tracts 1720–23*, ed. H. Davis (Blackwell, 1963), p. 341.

Academy of Modern Bedlam. And there, the dunce excusing his benighted specialization:

I meddle, Goddess! only in my Sphere[1]

would meet, in justice, all mankind as his true opposite:

All quit their Sphere, and rush into the skies.[2]

The criteria for admission are astonishingly diverse: who can escape certification? And among the reasons for declaring some men mad are prejudice of various kinds, and censorship of some sorts of intellectual inquiry and aspiration as absurd by definition.

If not all men, most: Augustan Bedlam bids fair to unpeople Europe, past and present. It is a hospital for incurables (endowed by ruined millionaires?) where Descartes would encounter Macedonia's madman, Alexander, and *all* other heroes, mad producers of those equal nonsenses, 'conquests' and 'systems'. Defoe and Sir Richard Blackmore would doze off to the sound of critical commentaries on their works resounding from 'an hundred head of Aristotle's friends'. Empedocles is hailed by innumerable creatures of bigotted zeal—Platonists, mystics, non-conformists, an astronomer who has taken on responsibility for the behaviour of the sun (the astronomer an almost unique example of cure). There are inmates scribbling on walls, imitating asses and monkeys, trying to regain sunbeams from cucumbers. There is a whole tribe of people with deranged vision, 'one of their eyes turn'd inwards, the other directly to the Zenith', not far from others humming and rocking, in unison with a preacher. Lucretius, Theobald, Charles the Twelfth, Ozell, Epicurus, Wotton, Colley Cibber; those excessively convinced of something, those excessively convinced of nothing. Equally deranged are a ceaseless irritable search for absolute contentment, in a mist of mirth and opium and tears, and the brazen brightness of heroic self-approval: 'What then remains? Ourself'.[3] Mad opinionatry, mad creativity, mad natural

---

[1] Pope, *The Dunciad* (1743), Book IV, l. 432.
[2] Pope, *An Essay on Man*, Epistle I, l. 124.
[3] *The Dunciad* (1743), Book I, l. 217.

science, the rage of innovation as the sole true mark of excellence,
side by side with a ponderous appeal to classical learning and classical values. The crowded mad of Pope and Swift seek Parnassian
status and recognition. They acquire their own metaphysics, an
adulterous blend of Aquinas and Descartes; their proper sociology,
theology, critical theory; their psychopathology, the vapours;
their natural history, butterfly markings and the numbered streaks
on tulips. So energetic and ambitious are they that their ultimate
victory seems assured. Meanwhile, they must be kept in—or,
rather, *out*:

> Shut, shut the door, good *John!* fatigu'd I said,
> Tye up the knocker, say I'm sick, I'm dead,
> The Dog-star rages! nay 'tis past a doubt,
> All *Bedlam*, or *Parnassus* is let out:
> Fire in each eye, and Papers in each hand,
> They rave, recite, and madden through the land.[1]

As seen from the top of Parnassus, the road of excess leads down-
hill to the Cave of Spleen; Twickenham keeps its distance from
the frenzied poets' cave. But Atticus reminds us of the iniquities of
Parnassian snobbery and malice; Addison and Colley Cibber join
in cultivating the 'proud Parnassian sneer'.[2] Bedlam *and* Parnassus,
Bedlam *or* Parnassus: the dunce and the idiot are trying to climb
the hill, or at least to fit out grottos of their own:

> Is there, who lock'd from Ink and Paper, scrawls
> With desp'rate Charcoal round his darken'd walls?[3]

They even seek redress for the traditional Parnassian injustice
inflicted on their supposed sweet humility:

> I intend to do justice upon our neighbours, inhabitants of the
> upper Parnassus, who, taking advantage of the rising ground,
> are perpetually throwing down rubbish, dirt, and stones upon

---

[1] Pope, *An Epistle to Dr. Arbuthnot*, ll. 1–6.
[2] See *An Epistle to Dr. Arbuthnot*, ll. 193–214, and *The Dunciad* (1743), Book II,
l. 5.
[3] *An Epistle to Dr. Arbuthnot*, ll. 19–20.

us, never suffering us to live in peace. These men, while they enjoy the crystal streams of Helicon, envy us our common water, which (thank our stars), though it is somewhat muddy, flows in much greater abundance. Nor is this the greatest injustice we have to complain of; for though it is evident that we never made the least attempt or inroad into *their* territories, but lived contented in our native fens, they have often not only committed petty larcenies upon our borders, but driven the country and carried off at once *whole cartloads* of our manufacture, to reclaim some of which stolen goods is part of the design of this treatise.[1]

Bad literature may be the satirist's compost. But the sinking theorist is being allowed to ask in comic form a question satire of such scope is bound to raise: what motivates the animus against its victims? To give a simple answer, whether in terms sympathetic to the satirist or unsympathetic, is to qualify as yet another dunce; but any answer needs to reckon with Augustan Bedlam as an Augustan edifice, built for the dunce-creator by the creator of the dunce.

It is a fabric of peculiar complexity, almost a folly in itself, with vast assembly halls loud with snoring and the clank of mimic Hectors, and random seminar rooms and studies linked by corridors that whisper good advice—'first follow Nature', 'shun extremes', 'believe in the unalterable fitness of things'. The walls are hung with texts the architects themselves supplied. There is Johnson declaring that we *know* our will is free, 'and *there's* an end on't', close to Pope rebuking those who are so stupid as to call in question 'two things the most self-evident, the Existence of our Soul, and the Freedom of our Will'.[2] Pope is quoted pointing the way back from perplexities to the simple truth about virtue and vice:

> Ask your own heart, and nothing is so plain;
> 'Tis to mistake them, costs the time and pain.[3]

---

[1] *The Art of Sinking in Poetry*, ch. 1.

[2] Boswell, *Life of Johnson* (Oxford, 1946), p. 388. Pope, *The Dunciad* (1743), Book IV, l. 481 n.

[3] *An Essay on Man*, Epistle II, ll. 215–16.

The inmates rejoice to find Johnson rebuking Swift for coining the paradox that men are 'grateful in the same degree as they are resentful', identifying it as a contribution to mischievous error, such as is sponsored by 'all those who confound the colours of right and wrong, and instead of helping to settle their boundaries, mix them with so much art, that no common mind is able to dis-unite them'.[1] In the Hall of Heroes, thronged with classical translators dressed in outsize armour, hang the opening lines of Pope's mercifully never-completed epic about Brutus:

> The Patient Chief, who lab'ring long, arriv'd
> On Britains Shore and brought with fav'ring Gods
> Arts Arms and Honour to her Ancient Sons:
> Daughter of Memory! from elder Time
> Recall; and me, with Britains Glory fir'd,
> Me, far from meaner Care or meaner Song,
> Snatch to thy holy Hill of Spotless Bay,
> My Country's Poet, to record her Fame.[2]

The true looks mock; duncely scepticism is sometimes rebuked as if it were scepticism itself that constitutes the fault; precipitating riddles and directing inquiry, reason can also be offered as their censor; the jokes and cynicism about modern heroics occur in a context where Parnassus apes classical epic but is at the same time quick to declare *all* heroes mad, all heroism lies and murder.

As a prescription for dull mock-heroic, of which the eighteenth century provides enough to pave the way as far back as Olympus, we could turn to some statement of static contrast between ancient and modern such as this by Swift:

> I desired that the senate of *Rome* might appear before me in one large Chamber, and an assembly of somewhat a latter age in counterview in another. The first seemed to be an assembly of heroes and demigods; the other a knot of pedlars, pickpockets, highway-men, and bullies.[3]

---

[1] *The Rambler*, no. 4, 31 March 1750.
[2] Pope, *Poems*, ed. J. Butt (Methuen, 1963), p. 836.
[3] *Gulliver's Travels*, Book III, ch. 7.

Far more provocative is the brisk relativism offered by Swift elsewhere:

> Whoe'er excels in what we prize
> Appears a Hero to our Eyes.[1]

What the sot and lunatic achieve by dreaming, the duncely pane-
gyrist artfully contrives by obeying what *The Art of Sinking* calls
'the Golden Rule of Transformation, which consists in converting
vices into their *bordering* virtues':

> A man who is a spendthrift and will not pay a just debt may
> have his injustice transformed into liberality; cowardice may be
> metamorphosed into prudence; intemperance into good nature
> and good fellowship; corruption into patriotism; and lewdness
> into tenderness and facility. (Chapter 14)

Swift ironically confirms the instruction:

> Is he to Avarice inclin'd?
> Extol him for his generous mind.[2]

The opposite categories make the satiric point against the lying
laureate; but Nature can work similar mutations:

> See anger, zeal and fortitude supply;
> Ev'n av'rice, prudence; sloth, philosophy;
> Lust, thro' some certain strainers well refin'd,
> Is gentle love, and charms all womankind:
> Envy, to which th'ignoble mind's a slave,
> Is emulation in the learn'd or brave:
> Nor Virtue, male or female, can we name,
> But what will grow on Pride, or grow on Shame.[3]

In *The Dunciad*, we might say, the sinker's rhetoric and the dark
proclivities of Nature are in league. Not enough of the poem's
complexity and force is conveyed if we content ourselves with

[1] 'Cadenus and Vanessa', ll. 732–3.
[2] 'Directions for a Birth-Day Song', ll. 123–4.
[3] *An Essay on Man*, Epistle I, ll. 187–94.

seeing it as the mirror of classical and Christian culture held up to contemporary endarkenment. But equally, the paradoxical account seems far too cheap—namely, that Pope is in this poem of the devil's (or, worse, the Absurdists') party without knowing it.

It might, however, be partly right to see *The Dunciad* as an exercise of projection, by means of which some of the inertness, the complacency, the classicizing, that are among the disappointing ingredients of Augustanism, are visited upon its enemies and given a meretricious life, but a life they might otherwise lack. We readily talk of what the poem's 'accelerated grimace' reveals of its own time.[1] Dulness herself incites her favourite hero, Cibber, to recognize the satire's deepest point in acknowledging that the teeming monsters of his world of Uncreation are not outside him, but occupy the Self:

> Son; what thou seek'st is in thee! Look, and find
> Each Monster meets its likeness in thy mind.
>
> (Book III. ll. 252–3)

But Colley and his monsters are all to be sought, however much they mirror of their time, in the mind of their creator, Pope.

A bizarre digression may help us here. There are the mirrored creatures of the state of contemplative ecstasy:

> Mean while the Mind, from pleasure less,
> Withdraws into its happiness:
> The Mind, that Ocean where each kind
> Does streight its own resemblance find;
> Yet it creates, transcending these,
> Far other Worlds, and other Seas;
> Annihilating all that's made
> To a green Thought in a green Shade.[2]

For Pope to acknowledge the monstrous deformities of *The Dunciad* by analogy with Marvell's recognition of inscrutable and

---

[1] The phrase is from Ezra Pound, 'Hugh Selwyn Mauberley'. *Personae* (Faber, 1952), p. 198.

[2] Marvell, 'The Garden'. *Poems*, ed. H. Macdonald (Routledge, 1952), p. 52.

transcendent creative powers in the mind would break the satirist's necessary fiction, that he represents in his work not what he finds in himself, but what there is to castigate in the world around him. It would also need the tragic honesty of another major poet's encounter with the mirror his own work provides:

> Those masterful images because complete
> Grew in pure mind, but out of what began?
> A mound of refuse or the sweepings of a street,
> Old kettles, old bottles, and a broken can,
> Old iron, old bones, old rags, that raving slut
> Who keeps the till. Now that my ladder's gone,
> I must lie down where all the ladders start,
> In the foul rag-and-bone shop of the heart.[1]

Whatever Pope might have been able to admit to himself concerning the place from which Colley and the dunces ascend their ladders of low sublimity, there is no room for the admission in *The Dunciad*. One reaches, as with Swift, a point at which uncertainty about how much he could understand and acknowledge of the felt impulses and pressures in his work is left relying on little more than intuition and hazardous speculation. These are, of course, limits to define and respect, rather than overrun with hopeful pathology.

Pope's character of the mad Atossa spares her no more than it spares us. But it shows a vibrant imaginative sense of her condition:

> No Thought advances, but her Eddy Brain
> Whisks it about, and down it goes again.[2]

His lofty mentor, Bolingbroke, complacently avails himself of the routine Augustan notion:

> I never met the madwoman at Brentford, decked out in old and
> new rags, and nice and fantastical in the manner of wearing

---

[1] Yeats, 'The Circus Animals' Desertion', ll. 33–40. *Collected Poems* (Macmillan, 1950), p. 392.

[2] *Moral Essays*, Epistle II, ll. 121–2.

them, without reflecting on many of the profound scholars, and sublime philosophers of our own, and of former ages.[1]

We would not expect either Pope or Bolingbroke to match—nor would they have admired—the audacity of Yeats:

> I sometimes compare myself with the mad old slum women I hear denouncing and remembering: 'How dare you,' I heard one of them say of some imaginary suitor, 'and you without health or a home!'[2]

But Pope grows restive in the face of Bolingbroke's display of genteel nonchalance towards his own feelings of incoherence and of despair about the self:

> You laugh, half Beau half Sloven if I stand,
> My Wig all powder, and all snuff my Band;
> You laugh, if Coat and Breeches strangely vary,
> White gloves, and Linnen worthy Lady Mary!
> But when no Prelate's Lawn with Hair-shirt lin'd,
> Is half so incoherent as my Mind,
> When (each Opinion with the next at strife,
> One ebb and flow of follies all my Life)
> I plant, root up, I build, and then confound,
> Turn round to square, and square again to round;
> You never change one muscle of your face,
> You think this Madness but a common case,
> Nor once to Chanc'ry, nor to Hales apply;
> Yet hang your lip, to see a Seam awry![3]

It is hard to find elsewhere such a playful witty mastery, so alert a social sense, consistent with a truly felt distress. Pope will not often so associate criticism of himself with attacks on customary victims —here, squalor and hypocrisy. It is a priceless moment. But it returns us to Johnson, in whom the true cost of so many of the

---

[1] *A Letter to Mr. Pope* (1751 edn.), p. 244.

[2] 'A General Introduction for my Work', *Essays and Introductions* (Macmillan, 1961), p. 521.

[3] *The First Epistle of the First Book of Horace Imitated*, ll. 161–74.

pressures of Augustan reason are felt and acknowledged in the context of a fear of going *in fact* insane:

> On Monday the 16. I sat for my picture, and walked a considerable way with little inconvenience. In the afternoon and evening I felt myself light and easy, and began to plan schemes of life. Thus I went to bed, and in a short time waked and sat up as has been long my custom, when I felt a confusion and indistinctness in my head which lasted, I suppose about half a minute; I was alarmed and prayed God, that however he might afflict my body he would spare my understanding. This prayer, that I might try the integrity of my faculties I made in Latin verse. The lines were not very good, but I knew them not to be very good, I made them easily, and concluded myself to be unimpaired in my faculties.[1]

[1] Letter to Mrs. Thrale, 19 June 1783. *Letters*, ed. R. W. Chapman (Oxford, 1952), Vol. III, p. 34.

IV

Sean O'Casey and Naturalism

J. A. SNOWDEN

A FAMILIAR critical cliché about O'Casey is that he began life as a Naturalist or Realist who wilfully abandoned Naturalism for experimental forms beyond his competence as a playwright. Robert Brustein, for example, expresses this view in its most extreme form:

> ... an extremely over rated writer with two or three Naturalist plays to his credit, followed by a lot of ideological bloat and embarrassing bombast ...[1]

It has always struck me, to begin with, that O'Casey was not strictly a Naturalist at all in his early trilogy and, if we insist on labelling his work 'Naturalist', we must do so with some reservation. In my view his Naturalism was, from the beginning, of a very different kind from that of the post-Ibsenite Naturalism of his contemporaries. It is therefore worth looking again at these early plays both for themselves and in the dramatic climate of their period, because much of the subsequent misconception about O'Casey's later development arises from a failure to understand the true nature of his earlier work.

From the earliest days of the Abbey theatre there was a gradual movement away from Yeats's poetic ideal towards a realistic peasant drama and, although it usually contained some 'criticism of life', there was little 'vision of life'. Fitzmaurice, Robinson, Colum and Murray, in their different ways, were the best known representatives of this school.

Their themes and characters were drawn from lower middle-class life in the Irish countryside. The land, money, marriage

[1] *The Theatre of Revolt* (Methuen, 1965), p. viii.

prospects, social esteem—all these in one form or another were the material on which they drew. Their dialogue was plain and naturalistic with the occasional flavour of Gaelic syntax or the odd metaphorical reminder of the countryside.

Gradually, as in the later plays of Robinson and Murray, language becomes so austere that it serves as the barest instrument of character and plot. Plot itself is increasingly concerned with the clash of mind and well within the confines of a domestic scene. Sometimes, as in *Maurice Harte*, it is concerned with the even narrower world of a mind's private struggle within itself.

To place O'Casey's early plays in the same genre as these 'realistic' plays seems to me a gross display of critical insensibility. Even so eminent a critic as Allardyce Nicoll writes: 'Mr. O'Casey's first works were cast in the realistic mould as modified by earlier Irish writers.'[1]

If we accept this judgement as a premise, we must accept the familiar argument that his later plays were not a natural extension of the earlier works but an unhappy experiment. The truth is, I believe, O'Casey has never been either intentionally or accitally a Realist in the post-Ibsenite sense.

'This headlong search or quiet scrutiny for realism, exact imitation of life in the drama has outwitted the critics into being puzzled over everything in a play that doesn't fit calmly into their poor spirit level and timid thumb rule.'[2]

As a poetic dramatist he was concerned not so much with reality as with the imaginative transformation of reality. It can be shown, of course, that most of his plays spring directly from his own experience of life. But his reading of life was essentially a poet's. His preparation as a dramatist owed as much to his wide reading of great literature as it did to a youth spent in the Dublin slums.

In every O'Casey play there is a dichotomy of reality and dream: the world that is and the world that might be.

[1] *British Drama* (Harrap, 1951), p. 484.
[2] *The Flying Wasp* (Macmillan, 1937), p. 117.

'Sacred heart of Jesus, take away our hearts o' stone and give us hearts o' flesh . .'[1]

These words of the bereaved Mrs. Boyle at the end of *Juno and the Paycock* remind us of the man who had resigned from the world of practical politics. It is no accident that O'Casey turned to drama after his disenchantment with the National movement. His own words strangely parallel the prophetic words of Yeats:

> Too long a sacrifice
> Can make a stone of the heart.[2]

Whereas the 'Realist' seeks to reveal reality, the poetic dramatist uses reality as the raw material for his dream. In Robinson's *White-headed Boy*, the climax is reached at the moment of self-realization when George discovers that he is not, after all, fitted to be a medical student but would be happier as a general labourer. A discovery such as his is the usual ingredient in the theatre of Realism; when it arrives too late, as in *The Clancy Name*, the outcome is tragedy. To the Realist what matters is the clarification of reality to the group or the individual.

In the plays of Sean O'Casey there is no climax leading to a neat resolution of the problem. There cannot be, for his purpose is social, not psychological or domestic. No reformation for Captain Boyle or Fluther Good is possible while society is organized in its present form. For this reason the dramatist's presentation of reality carries implications of the dream, of the world as it might be.

In his first successful play, he uses as a basis the familiar Irish myth-making so successfully exploited by Lady Gregory and by Synge in *The Playboy of the Western World*. Donal Davoren basks in the reputation others have created for him but, unlike Christy Mahon in Synge's play, he is not transformed by the myth: he is still as cowardly and ineffectual at the end as he was in the beginning.

[1] *Collected Plays*, Vol. I, p. 87.
[2] *Collected Poems* (Macmillan, 1950), p. 202.

Indeed in these early O'Casey plays there is never any evolution or transformation in the characters. They stand out, for the most part, as memorable grotesques in the Dickens manner. The dramatist's visualization of his characters in these plays bears a striking resemblance to Dickens's own method.[1] If we compare two random sets of such description, the first pair from O'Casey, the second from Dickens, we can see that the resemblance is very close:

1(a) ... He is a man of about sixty ... His neck is short, and his head looks like a stone ball that one sometimes sees on top of a gatepost...[2]

(b) His face is like a bundle of crinkled paper ... He has a habit of constantly shrugging his shoulders with a peculiar twitching movement, meant to be ingratiating. His face is invariably ornamented with a grin...[3]

2(a) A big loud man with a stare, and a metallic laugh. A man made out of coarse material, which seemed to have been stretched to make so much of him ... A man with a pervading appearance on him of being inflated like a balloon and ready to start...[4]

(b) But what added most to the grotesque expression of his face, was a ghastly smile, which, appearing to be the mere result of habit and to have no connection with any mirthful feeling ... gave him the aspect of a panting dog...[5]

All four of these random descriptions have certain characteristics in common. All describe the human being as something other than human: sometimes as an inert object—'a stone ball', 'a bundle of crinkled paper', 'like a balloon'—or as an animal—'the aspect of a panting dog'. They catch the human face or gesture in a fixed and frozen attitude—'invariably ornamented with a grin', 'the

---

[1] I am not concerned here (*pace* Raymond Williams) with the theatrical validity of O'Casey's practice, only with his intention. See p. 62, n.1.

[2] *Collected Plays*, Vol. I, p. 9.

[3] Op. cit., p. 10.

[4] *Hard Times* (Oxford), p. 14.

[5] *The Old Curiosity Shop* (Oxford), p. 22.

mere result of habit'. They are deliberate exaggerations, though they are also the result of an unusually keen observation of real models—a faculty which Dickens and O'Casey shared in large measure.

The characters in these early plays are not so much individuals in a particular situation as social caricatures drawn several times larger than life. Tommy Owens's imbecile patriotism, Minnie Powell's naïvety, or Grigson's Orange Bible-thumping are intentional exaggerations. The playwright's sympathy for them is a social sympathy. In the stage directions, he writes of Davoren:

> His struggle through life had been a hard one and his efforts have been handicapped by an inherited and self-developed devotion to the might of design, the mystery of colour . . .[1]

Of Minnie Powell, he writes:

> . . . the fact of being forced to earn her living, and to take care of herself, on account of her parents' early death, has given her a force and an assurance beyond her years . . .[2]

What we are witnessing in these plays is not naturalistic or realistic drama as it is commonly understood but a kind of social abstract in which the microcosm on the stage reflects the macrocosm without. Pattern, therefore, and not plot is the cohesive force in the action.

Critical objections to O'Casey's structure have nearly always been based on naturalistic criteria and have generally been directed to the playwright's failure to tie together the threads of the plot. I think they almost always miss the point.

O'Casey's plays are held together not so much by plot as by pattern. In *The Shadow of a Gunman*, for instance, the news of the death of Maguire at the end of Act 1 is neatly paralleled by the death of Minnie Powell at the end of Act 2. In each case the contrasting effect of the event on Davoren is carefully underlined.

[1] Op. cit., p. 93.
[2] Op. cit., p. 105.

Similarly, in *Juno and the Paycock*, Mrs. Tancred's agony at the loss of her son has its precise counterpart in the closing minutes of the play when Mrs. Boyle is informed of the death of her own son. To emphasize their common tragedy, Mrs. Boyle recalls the earlier bereavement and repeats Mrs. Tancred's prayer.

Ibsen is generally held to be the father of modern Naturalism in the theatre, though, of course, Naturalism of setting had preceded his arrival on the English stage. He was, however, almost certainly responsible for originating that special brand of anti-Romantic Naturalism that became such a pervasive influence in European drama.

He was at one time chiefly known in England as the author of psychological and 'problem' plays of which *A Doll's House* and *Ghosts*[1] were the best known. Although these plays had characteristics peculiar to Ibsen's own dramatic method, there is little doubt that essentially his aims and methods were widely imitated, even by Abbey theatre dramatists like Murray and Robinson.

It is revealing to compare a prototype such as *A Doll's House* with O'Casey's early plays to discover how much the two playwrights had in common and how much they differed. Certainly they were both 'Realists' in so far as they attempted honestly to communicate their own particular vision of life, without allowing considerations of artistic fashion to interfere with that communication. Given the terms and conditions laid down by the dramatists themselves, the outcome of an Ibsen play and that of an early O'Casey play has an inevitability that excludes popular taste or dramatic fashion.

There is another similarity between, say, *A Doll's House* and any early O'Casey play: both employed stock characters and situations which were part of their dramatic inheritance. The action and outcome of Ibsen's play turns upon Krogstadt's fatal letter; the action of *Juno and the Paycock* is largely determined by a

---

[1] I am here only concerned with certain aspects of these plays which were imitated by the later Naturalists. Ibsen, both in his earlier and later phases, wrote very different kinds of plays from the two mentioned here. It is certainly no longer true that his more symbolic and poetic drama is less well known.

will. The agents of these respective documents, Krogstadt and Bentham, are in different ways stock villains of the nineteenth-century theatre. The former, a sinister interloper, makes his unwelcome appearance against the idyllic background of a children's party. The smooth-talking Bentham is the seducer of the Innocent Mary.

There is nothing very surprising about this and, indeed, the whole Naturalistic theatre has relied heavily on character and situation inherited from earlier traditions in the drama. Raymond Williams sees Naturalism as being merely a limited rejection of the Romantic theatre:

> ... It is in this respect that one must emphasize that Naturalism is a legitimate child of the romantic drama; a child which makes a limited rejection of its parent but which remains essentially formed by its general inheritance . . .[1]

Again, both O'Casey and Ibsen, though they wrote within the conventions of Naturalism found that convention somewhat limiting. The theme of *A Doll's House* is heavily underlined at appropriate moments of the play by the use of symbolism. The masquerade dress, the bird symbolism, Dr. Rank and the visiting card—the whole play is shot through with symbolism, both verbal and concrete, which takes us to the inner core of the play's meaning in a way that mere truth-to-life dialogue would never achieve.

In O'Casey's first plays there is considerable symbolic content of a kind similar to Ibsen's. The titles themselves (as with *A Doll's House* and *Ghosts*) have been carefully chosen for their symbolic suggestiveness. *The Plough and the Stars* is symbolically at the centre of O'Casey's great theme of the world that is and the world that might be.

Uncle Peter's ostrich plume suggests perhaps the traditional posture of the ostrich burying its head in the sand—a message not only of particular application but central to the whole meaning of the play. The incident concerning the votive light in *Juno*, though

[1] *Drama from Ibsen to Eliot* (Chatto and Windus, 1965), p. 69.

somewhat more horrific in its effects, is a presage of a coming event of the same nature as Dr. Rank's visiting card.

There is, too, in the work of both dramatists a strong, coherent, verbal organization of their respective themes through the use of irony, repetition and parallelism—a unity of language beyond mere truth-to-life dialogue.

Here, however, Ibsen and O'Casey part company. Structurally there is an enormous difference between their work for their aims are quite different. Ibsen is rigidly deterministic. Each part of his pattern is more tightly woven into the fabric than it is in any of O'Casey's plays.

He proceeds by a series of revelations through the dialogue in which the characters reveal more and more about themselves and their relationship. It is not until the last act of *A Doll's House*, when Helmer discovers the full story of his wife's contract with the sinister Krogstadt, that Nora comes to a full realization that their marriage is doomed.

Ibsen's tightness of structure can be seen most clearly in his method of revealing the past only through the dialogue. Since the past in an Ibsen drama plays such a crucial part in an understanding of the present, this retrospective technique is central to his dramatic method. One must admire the skill and naturalness of a good deal of this and his drama gains enormously in concentration as a consequence.

Nevertheless, some of it now appears somewhat forced recapitulation of the past as when Krogstadt, in his second appearance, reveals to the audience details of the loan contracted by Nora:

> When your husband was ill, you came to me to borrow twelve hundred dollars . . . I promised to find you the money, on certain conditions. You were so taken up at the time with your husband's illness, and so eager to have the wherewithal for your journey, that you probably did not give much thought to the details. Allow me to remind you of them . . .[1]

One feels, all the same, that Nora does not really need to be reminded of the details for they are facts that she already knows too

[1] *Seven Famous Plays* (Duckworth, 1950), p. 42.

well. Krogstadt is talking not so much for Nora's information as for the information of the audience. Perhaps, however, one should not object to a small loss of credibility when it is so well compensated by a gain in compression.

It does illustrate, nevertheless, Ibsen's concern for tightness of structure. Indeed, so tightly is the play organized that it becomes impossible to speak of character, plot and dialogue as separate elements. The entrance of a character signals new knowledge of the past and thereby an advance on the present action.

Ibsen's characters are interlocked in an intimate inner world of their own. Their past relationships have a bearing on their present relationships and each is an agent in the total revelation. In the end the concentration goes even further for all the characters and all the revelations they make are directed to Nora's self-revelation.

The only occasions, five in all, that Ibsen employs the soliloquy are at different stages when he wishes to show us Nora's reactions to the progress of events. Not until that final soliloquy, at the point where Helmer has taken the letter from the box, does she realize that their marriage is irredeemably lost.

Now, although this special retrospective method may be exclusively Ibsen's, nevertheless, this aim of psychological revelation or the growth of awareness seems to me to be a common factor in Naturalist drama of the present century. The drama in *A Doll's House* resides more in the growth of awareness in the mind of a single character, Nora, than it does in the problem or the discussion. All the other elements—plot, characterization and language—are merely agents in this process. It remains, of course, a 'problem' play in the sense that Ibsen poses a problem for the audience. What Nora did with her new-found awareness certainly constituted a problem for the audiences who first witnessed the play.

In further contrast with Sean O'Casey, Ibsen develops his theme against a background of seeming objectivity. Compare, for example, the opening stage directions of *A Doll's House* with those of *The Plough and the Stars*. Ibsen reads:

A room comfortably and tastefully but not expensively furnished. In the back on the right a door leads to the hall; on the left another door leads to the study. Between the two doors, a pianoforte . . .[1]

O'Casey reads:

> The home of the Clitheroes. It consists of the front and back drawing rooms in a fine Georgian house, struggling for its life against the assaults of time and the more savage assaults of the tenants . . . The room directly in front of the audience is furnished in a way that suggests an attempt towards a finer expression of domestic life . . .[2]

We can perceive in those very first stage directions an essential difference that runs right through the respective plays. Ibsen's words are flat, objective. He takes up no position but leaves the unfolding of the play to reveal, piece by piece, the reality behind the appearance. Not infrequently after the last veil has been lifted one is left with some imperfectly explained puzzle—'the miracle of miracles'. It is essentially the drama of inwardness.

O'Casey's opening words, on the other hand, are indicative of an attitude to his art that is diametrically opposed to modern Naturalism. His is the attitude of the outraged poet, commenting as well as describing. There are no hidden secrets. Everything is fully conceived and is seen to be such. If Ibsen's tense is the past in the present, O'Casey's is the continuous present.

The contemporaneity of O'Casey's early trilogy has often been stressed. These plays dealt with great events in the very recent past, events witnessed by the audiences who watched them at their first performances at the Abbey theatre. But there is another quality besides their contemporaneity: the sense of the actual.

Now, this sense of the actual, the illusion that what we are witnessing is living and growing before our eyes, is created mainly by the force of the language. It is not only through O'Casey's use of repetitions, distinguishing phrases or even through the

[1] Op. cit., p. 19.
[2] Op. cit., p. 161.

faithful imitation of dialect that this illusion is established in the mind.

The illusion is established because the language itself is the determining force of everything else in the play. If we consider the opening scene of *The Plough and the Stars* we can see amply illustrated O'Casey's method of employing dialogue and how radically it differs from the normal Naturalistic method.

The conversation between Mrs Gogan and Fluther is functional in that it gives us some basic information about Nora and Jack Clitheroe and their present relationship. But it does much more than this. It sets the mood for the whole play. Most of it consists of a kind of verbal tennis in which the language moves back and forth, without providing information or advancing the action. Some of it stands still while the characters philosophize or merely comment on what takes their fancy at that moment in time. Thus, while the irascible Peter Flynn is getting dressed in his Foresters' uniform, Mrs Gogan comments:

> Isn't oul' Peter a funny-lookin' little man . . . like something you'd pick off a Christmas tree.[1]

Or again, when she and Fluther notice 'The Sleepin' Vennis', the incident and the conversation bear little relation to the plot or the action of the play.

The life of a traditional Naturalistic play resides not so much in the language as in the firm cohesion of all the elements. The plot concerning the will in *Juno and the Paycock* could be omitted without destroying the essential structure of the play since its structure depends more on pattern than on plot. Its existence is not central to O'Casey's dramatic design. The fateful letter in the box in *A Doll's House* or the telegram in *The Whiteheaded Boy* are, however, essential elements in the plot and dramatic design of those plays. They are part of the mechanism of suspense and activate the final dénouement.

O'Casey's plays differ fundamentally from most Naturalist drama in the present century by a quality of what I would call

[1] Op. cit., p. 166.

'outwardness'—a quality which links him to earlier forms of drama and has had the effect of making his plays appear unfamiliar to the modern theatregoer and critic. This quality of explicitness is seen, for example, in Elizabethan theatre in the way that characters explain in detail their inward sensations and emotions.

Where a modern dramatist might leave us to observe or deduce the effects of Olivia's sudden infatuation for Viola in *Twelfth Night*, Shakespeare spells it out in detail:

> How now?
> Even so quickly may one catch the plague?
> Methinks I feel this youth's perfections
> With an invisible and subtle stealth
> To creep in at mine eyes.[1]

Explicitness is seen at its most dramatic when a character is about to die or fall from fortune. In this way Bessie Burgess's death is played out in full explicit language:

> There's a fire burnin' in me blood . . . Jesus Christ me sight's goin'! It's all dark, dark! Nora, hold me hand! . . . I'm dyin' . . . I feel it . . . Oh God, oh God . . .[2]

More recent experiments in what is loosely called the Theatre of the Absurd have implied an extreme rejection of Naturalism. Language is incoherent and inconsecutive, reflecting a world without meaning and man in isolation from his fellows. Characters like Davies in *The Caretaker* or Bérenger in *Rhinoceros* are chosen for their anonymity or inarticulateness. They live in a world, disconnected, meaningless and terrifyingly hostile. In spite of its implied rejection of Naturalism, however, it has always seemed to me to be merely an exaggeration of a tendency already inherent in Naturalism, namely, the qualities of understatement and inwardness.

O'Casey is at the opposite pole, for his drama implies a common cultural tradition, both literary and popular. His world is

[1] I.v. 263–7. The London Shakespeare, ed. J. Munro (1958), Vol. II, p. 707.
[2] Op. cit., p. 259.

articulate—some might say too articulate—striving towards per-fectability, order and progress. He believed that literature ought to be a celebration of life and that drama was a part of literature.

To some extent the unique form that his theatre took is a re-flection of his own struggle from squalid obscurity to international recognition as a great playwright. At the same time it was deter-mined by the direction that his own reading took.

As a young man he had little experience of the modern move-ment of Realism. Almost the only theatre where he could have seen representative examples was the Abbey which, according to his own testimony, he had visited 'but twice'.[1] The dramatist he knew and admired most was Shakespeare whose influence was obviously profound and lifelong. Of modern dramatists the one he admired most was Shaw, not only for his ideology but because Shaw, to some degree, belonged to the tradition of the drama as literature.

As he came to write plays rather later in life than most other successful playwrights, after some disenchantment with the aims and actions of Irish politicians, the drama became a unique forum in which he, the artist, could refashion the world neglected or misunderstood by the politician. The outward, expansive form that it took was an expression of what he had seen and what he had read.

[1] *Autobiographies*, Vol. II (Macmillan, 1963), p. 96.

V

Brendan Behan's 'The Hostage'[1]

JOHANNES KLEINSTÜCK

BRENDAN BEHAN did not leave any extensive work behind him: two plays, one novel, some books of sketches and memories. His relatively small productivity as an artist is not to be explained by the fact that he died too early; he was not, in himself, immature, nor did he suffer from what we sometimes call a loss of words, for this disease is not prevalent in Ireland. Indeed, according to his companion and biographer Rae Jeffs, Behan was full of stories, easily understood by the uninitiated, particularly those stories and songs which so frequently interrupt his narratives and of which he mastered an immense amount.[2] It was his way of living which prevented his writing. Of the forty years of his life (from 1923 to 1964) even Behan might not have been able to reckon how much time was spent in taverns. Moreover, he spent about eight years behind bars, for while he was still an adolescent he entangled himself in the muddle of Irish politics—not as a politician but as a fighter for the unity and liberty of his native island. He became a member of the I.R.A., long an illegal organization in Eire; and it was his intention to blow up a warship in Liverpool docks which first brought him to trial and to subsequent imprisonment in a Borstal (that prison without real bars). Yet even after his return to his birthplace, Dublin, he did not cease rebelling, as he describes for us in *Borstal Boy* (1958). For there he came into conflict with the law again, and even when he was finally released he rarely

[1] This essay was originally part of an informal birthday tribute to Professor Ludwig Borinski (11 January, 1970); the present translation is by R. Hausen.

[2] See the Introduction to *Confessions of an Irish Rebel* (1965), (Arrow Book paperback, 1967). The text was tape-recorded by Behan and published by Rae Jeffs. References are to the Arrow Book ed.; as here, p. 8.

practised his occupation as a painter, but roamed about Ireland France and England (where he was once again imprisoned).

Behan wrote only in order to make money, as he himself asserted.[1] Nevertheless he enjoyed his fame as a writer and liked to pose as the wild Irishman. This aspect of him is appreciated by the English, while the Irish disapprove of it. (If I may be allowed a personal comment—I was told in Ireland in 1962 that he was by no means considered a national hero, rather a 'villain', a word which seems archaic to us but which is well known there—yet I have heard other opinions too.)

Brendan Behan played a part, that of the rebel, of the outsider who despises laws and conventions. He played, one might say, the stage Irishman, and, according to report, he played the role well. He did not consider himself to be an artist. Joyce, whom Behan seems to have revered, wrote a book on the experience of becoming an artist, in which he became tenderly engrossed in his own youthful portrait, enjoying and conveying the melody of his own early verse. Behan abstained from that kind of self-glorification. When he talks about himself he is interested in Guinness and whiskey, abundant food, splendid talk with farmers on the West Coast, and his own proud past as a defender of Irish liberty, or the impertinent answers that he gave his judges and jailors. He is not interested, however, in how his own books came about, what he felt, or what he wanted to say in them. He talks of experience, of what is around him, of what is going on inside him, just as Yeats (in his *Autobiographies*) abstains from the interpretation of himself or his works.

Behan might have rejected, perhaps angrily, such comparison with Yeats. For Behan's origins were in the proletariat, whereas Yeats admired the society of the Great House and aspired to be an aristocrat—but even Yeats was often accused of posing, so that Lennox Robinson, in defence of him, said:

[H]is pose would have been to try and pass himself off as an ordinary man.[2]

[1] *Confessions*, p. 135.
[2] *Scattering Branches, Tributes to the Memory of W. B. Yeats*, ed. Stephen Gwynn (1940), p. 58.

Behan, at least partially, may be likened to that ideal writer addressed by Yeats in his valedictory poem:

> Sing the peasantry, and then
> Hard-riding country gentlemen,
> The holiness of monks, and after
> Porter-drinkers' ready laughter;
> Cast your mind on other days
> That we in coming days may be
> Still the indomitable Irishry.[1]

Behan belongs to the 'indomitable Irishry', though he did not want to have anything to do with country gentlemen. However, he did not move only within the circle of the proletariat but also within that which is called, in French, *le milieu*. Both had strong associations for him; for he grew up in a flat adjacent to a kind of brothel:

> It wasn't much of a brothel, God knows, but the inhabitants enjoyed themselves or seemed so, I think they did more drinking there than anything else; it was more a shebeen than a kip, kip being the Dublin word for a brothel and shebeen the Irish for a place where people are able to drink after hours.[2]

To this milieu Behan transferred the plot of his play *The Hostage*. First written in Irish, as he tells us in his *Irish Sketch Book*, it was performed, as *An Giall*, at the Damer Hall, St. Stephen's Green, Dublin in 1957.[3] The first English production followed on 14 October, 1958 at Joan Littlewood's Theatre Royal, Stratford, London E.15.[4] The play's location, according to the text, is 'an old house in Dublin'; the *Sketch Book* tells us that we should envisage this house to be in Nelson Street, near to Nelson's Pillar—

---

[1] *Collected Poems* (1952), p. 400.

[2] *Confessions*, p. 142.

[3] See *Brendan Behan's Island, An Irish Sketch Book* (1962), (Corgi Books, 1965). References are to the latter edition; as here, p. 17.

[4] Quotations are from the edition in *Methuen's Modern Plays*, ed. John Cullen, 1962).

since then, of course, blown up by the still active I.R.A.[1] The
house is built in Georgian style and has seen better times, so, it is
said, have its present occupants (p. 1). Pat, the manager, had
earlier fought for Ireland's liberty, and having lost a leg in the
process is only too ready to talk about his heroic past. His former
superior and brother in arms lives solely in the past, devises ima-
ginary battle plans, wears a kilt, makes a bagpipe resound now
and then, and, if he could have his way, would dispense with the
use of English and speak nothing but Irish—but which Irishmen
would understand him? Thus, in order to avoid the English and
unpatriotic Mister he calls himself Monsewer. We are not sur-
prised to learn that he is English on his father's side, and that he is
the only member of this circle of aristocratic descent; but he ignores his origin in the same way that he ignores the present time
(pp. 13–14). We live in the age of the atom bomb, and in Pat's
opinion this makes the I.R.A., or any other force, useless, whether
they are 'the Coldstream Guards, the Scots Guards, the Welsh
Guards, the Grenadier Guards and the bloody fire guards' (p. 5).
Yet the I.R.A. is not diverted in its activity by such realization.
In Belfast one of their soldiers (whom some would call a terrorist)
has been imprisoned and sentenced to death by hanging on the
following morning. As a counter-move the I.R.A. have abducted
a young English soldier, Leslie Williams, holding him as a hostage, to be shot in reprisal if the sentence is not amended. To Pat's
great annoyance two I.R.A. volunteers quarter the hostage in the
house which Pat manages, and keep a close guard on their captive.

From this situation the plot of the play is developed, and
occupies the few hours of the prisoner's detention. The inhabitants of the house receive Leslie in a friendly fashion, provide him
with cigarettes, beer (Guinness, of course), tea, and readings from
the Bible: Teresa, the country-bred, convent-educated, maid-ser-
vant even offers him her love. But Leslie is killed when the
house is besieged by the Irish police, tipped off by an informer. No
one knows whose bullet killed him. It is not even clear if he is

---

[1] The blow-up which took place in 1965 caused the following exchange:
'What's the difference between Napoleon and Nelson?' *Answer*: 'Napoleon was
Bonaparte and Nelson was blown apart.'

dead, in one sense, since he stands up, enveloped in a ghostly green
light, and sings:

> The bells of hell,
> Go ting-a-ling-a-ling,
> For you but not for me,
> O death, where is thy sting-a-ling-a-ling,
> Or grave thy victory?

At the close of the play all sing together; indeed, the audience
has joined in on several occasions.[1]

Many an English audience will have felt this play to be 'very
mad and very Irish'; indeed, it is only comprehensible from the
standpoint of a knowledge of Irish history. For one needs to recall that the Anglo-Irish conflict began in the twelfth century,
when the English—or more strictly, the Normans—began their
settlement on Irish shores before gradually extending their rule
over the whole island. The struggle seemed over in 1921. Michael
Collins, the leader of the Irish rebels, signed a treaty which left the
six northern counties, most of them predominantly Protestant,
still within the British Commonwealth, while the rest, mainly
Catholic, achieved independence. This seemed a reasonable
solution to many people—to many, but not to all. The radicals
continued to fight, and Michael Collins, more than anyone else
a national hero, was ambushed and killed.[2] The I.R.A., an illegal
and underground organization, still fights today for the liberation
of the six counties, whose inhabitants—and not only the Protes-
tants among them—resist such liberation strongly.[3]

This extraordinarily complex situation must be understood as
the necessary basis for an understanding of Behan's play, whose

[1] See the report of Richard Friedenthal in the *Welt* for 7 November, 1958:
according to him Brendan Behan on the first night contributed a tipsy song and
dance at the end to the audience's applause.

[2] See, Frank O'Connor, *The Big Fellow—Michael Collins and the Irish Revolu-
tion*, first published in 1937 entitled *Death in Dublin—Michael Collins and the
Irish Republic* (rev. ed., 1965, then Corgi Books, 1969).

[3] See a report in *Le Monde Hebdomadaire* (11 to 17 September, 1969), by Jacques
Amalric. According to him not even Bernadette Devlin, M.P., wants 'à tout
prix la réunification de l'Irlande' ('L'Ulster menacé de mort', III).

author found it necessary to expound upon the problem through dramatic dialogues. Pat, the former hero, who belongs with those unable to accept the treaty, is the play's spokesman: Meg, 'his consort', Colette, the young whore, and Ropeen, the old, listen to him, and let fall their remarks:

Pat: Five years' hard fighting.
Colette: Ah, God help us.
Ropeen: Heavy and many is the good man that was killed.
Pat: We had the victory—till they signed that curse-of-God treaty in London. They sold the six counties to England and Irishmen were forced to swear an oath of allegiance to the British Crown.
Meg: I don't know about the counties, but the swearing wouldn't come so hard on you.
Ropeen: Whatever made them do it, Mr. Pat?
Pat: Well, I'll tell you, Ropeen. It was Lloyd George and Birkenhead made a fool of Michael Collins and he signed an agreement to have no more fighting with England.
Meg: Then he should have been shot.
Pat: He was.
Meg: Ah, the poor man.

And then Pat is asked to sing the song of Michael Collins, the 'Laughing Boy', and he willingly does so (pp. 15–16).

No mention is made of the fact that the Six Counties did not want to become a part of the Irish Free State; that they were not sold, as Pat says. It is a matter of fact that the majority of Northern Irishmen remains faithful to the Union Jack. Diehards, if at all, recognize this very unhappily, and Brendan Behan does not go into the matter deeply.[1] Perhaps this does not surprise us. It is, however, strange that in this dialogue he turns such events into comedy, thereby ridiculing his own I.R.A. activities as well. He has gained a different point of view, yet without wholly rejecting his own patriotism.

In the *Sketch Book* he writes about the famine of 1847, for which he holds the English responsible:

[1] See the account of his activity in Northern Ireland (*Confessions*, pp. 154 ff.), and the paragraph 'The Black North' in *Sketch Book*, p. 157.

The greatest disaster to happen to any one nation in Europe, until the murder of six million Jews in the last war, was the Irish famine of 1847. Eight million people lived in Ireland at the time, but when the famine ended there were only four million left.

Behan accuses the English of mass murder, comparable in scale with the German one, and he continues, with bitter sarcasm:

> Queen Victoria was very distressed at the famine among her loyal subjects and she sent £5 to the Famine Relief Fund; then in case she might be thought to be showing open sympathies with a crowd of rebels, she sent £5 to the Battersea Dogs' Home.[1]

In *The Hostage* the English soldier, Leslie Williams, asks for what crime he is to be shot, and Pat explains:

> I'll tell you what you've done. Some time ago there was a famine in this country and people were dying all over the place. Well, your Queen Victoria, or whatever her bloody name was, sent five pounds to the famine fund and at the same time she sent five pounds to the Battersea Dogs' Home so no one could accuse her of rebel sympathies. (p. 87)

The same story, in almost the same words, but their meaning is different. In order to ensure that the tale is not taken too seriously the dramatist makes Meg comment:

> Good God, Pat, that was when Moses was in the Fire Brigade.

Since the play was written before the *Sketch Book* we cannot say that the author has changed his mind. He was, however, capable of revising his opinions in the light of facts, and could look ironically at convictions which had compelled him to fight. In this play Behan faced his own past, and with it part of his nature; and he found both were comic.

[1] *Sketch Book*, pp. 185–6.

F

Throughout the play the plot is controlled by a distancing irony, already perceptible in the description of the scene:

> Since the action of the play runs throughout the whole house and it isn't feasible to build it on stage, the setting is designed to represent one room of the house with a window overlooking the street. Leading off from this room are two doors and a staircase leading to the upper part. Between the room and the audience is an area that represents a corridor, a landing, or another room in the house and also serves as an extension of the room when the characters need room to dance and fight in. (p. 1)

No attempt is made to create illusions; from the start we know that this is no drama of naturalism, no drama, that is, concerned to give the appearance of reality. Consequently, the action does not aim at illusions either; obviously the characters speak colloquialisms, but one might take this opportunity of remarking that the playwright controls this manner of speech; moreover, the characters do not hesitate to do what a theorist of the classic theatre would censure, that is, they play outside their rôles, they address the audience, break into song and dance; yet, despite all this, they do not forget themselves, because it has been made clear from the beginning that they are playing a rôle, and do not intend to try to persuade an audience that they are doing otherwise.

Shall we then add this play to those categorized as epic theatre, acknowledge in it the 'alienation' effect, and assume the influence of Brecht? This would be wrong, for Behan does not use the theatre as a means to an end, however much he shares with Brecht certain formal elements in their use of theatre. Behan does not wish to teach an ideology, nor call upon the world to change in the cause of socialism. Therefore, he neither sums up morally nor requires his audience to reflect in any dogmatic way; he does not show how, ideally, things might be improved, but presents what he observes; he is interested in human events, not in theoretical inferences or conclusions.

Behan thus continues the tradition of the Irish Theatre movement in the way in which it was founded and practised by Yeats and Synge, though he is, perhaps, unaware of this. His final song celebrates the triumph of life over death, in which the Christian belief in salvation is partly parodied, partly affirmed. It would have been very easy indeed to have provided elevating songs of mutual understanding and peace among the peoples instead! This would have been not only easy but even obvious, because the play moves towards such a message and seems to contain it. The English soldier is not presented as a stranger, or an enemy, within the Irish environment, but seems to belong to it at once. At the end of the first Act he is pushed on to the stage where communal dancing is taking place, and with his very first words he adapts himself:

Don't stop. I like dancing.

He feels at home immediately. So much so that when the I.R.A. officer orders him to be silent he pays no attention but sings:

There's no place on earth like the world,
There's no place wherever you be. (p. 41)

All join in with him. The community of feeling is established without questioning. Why should a young Englishman have objections against the Irish, and vice versa? It is ridiculous to reproach him with wrongs committed in earlier times by his fellow-countrymen. For, on the one hand, the past has gone for ever, and on the other hand, it was the English landlords who were guilty of causing the misery of the Irish in the nineteenth century; and though they were his fellow-countrymen, they were members of a different caste, of a ruling class by which he is still ruled. He is an underdog, every bit as much as are the inhabitants of this house in Dublin. Among simple people of all nations mutual understanding should not be difficult to achieve.

The proletarian Brendan Behan sympathizes with the labouring class, whom he called 'the only real people'—in Dublin at least; and he even went so far as to assert that only 'the generals and the politicians' are interested in warfare,[1] though this is difficult to

[1] Ibid., p. 19 and p. 16.

accept in the light of his own activity in the I.R.A. Obviously, in some respects, Behan is again close in outlook to Brecht; but Behan does not believe in the doctrine of the 'election' of the working class; above all, he is indifferent to notions of class-consciousness. He likes labourers because he can talk and drink with them easily. Similarly, he also likes farmers, and British soldiers, above all the brave,[1] and he even feels benevolence towards the 'Earl of Birkenhead, who by all acounts was a very charming man and an alcoholic like myself';[2] Behan's humanity is not dictated by abstract principles. Thus the girl, Teresa, a devout Catholic, falls in love with the English soldier, Leslie, a Protestant. She puts a medal with the image of the Virgin round his neck, which he will carry for love of her (p. 70). Love and sympathy do not obey either frontiers or principles, and therefore the common people are not, in principle, philanthropic in general terms. Leslie sings:

I love my dear old Notting Hill, wherever I may roam,
But I wish the Irish and the niggers and the wogs,
Were kicked out and sent back home. (p. 78)

Behan sees no reason why Leslie's wishes should be corrected, as if they represented a false ideology. He accepts men, even the mad Monsewer, and only the fanatical I.R.A. officer cuts a bad figure, perhaps the worst in the whole play (pp. 49–50).

Men, and the world, are accepted. This is what marks the difference between the radical Behan and Brecht and all other Marxists, who had to condemn the play as pessimistic and defeatist. The threat of the atom bomb is ever-present, yet nobody complains, nobody expects, hopefully, a disarmament conference. The fate of the young rebel in Belfast is sealed from the start, as Pat acknowledges steadfastly:

Tomorrow morning at the hour of eight,
He'll hang as high as Killymanjaro. (p.3)

[1] *Confessions*, p. 116.
[2] Ibid., p. 100.

Such will be Leslie's fate whatever friendship he is offered, and he
knows that nobody can save him:

> You're as barmy as him if you think what's happening to me is
> upsetting the British Government. I suppose you think they're
> all sitting round in their West End clubs with handkerchiefs
> over their eyes, dropping tears into their double whiskies.
> (p. 89)

The fatalistic consciousness of the unavoidable gives the play a
tragic tone which pierces the grotesque and comic formulation
of its detail. Leslie is given the tragic status of a hero who atones
for a guilt which is not of his making but which he bears on be-
half of a remote, scarcely probable, past. For a moment the tragic
form gains the upper hand. Leslie lies there shot; Teresa bends
over him, and says:

> He died in a strange land, and at home he had no one.
> I'll never forget you, Leslie, till the end of time. (p. 108)

And then, all of a sudden, the appropriate requiem turns into a
celebration of life. Comedy overcomes tragedy; the 'play' its
seriousness. And looking back we recognize, retrospectively, that
the tragic tone was never more than an overtone, that the fatalism
always dissolved into comedy, and that all the burden, the pressure, of the past evanesced in a prevailing irony. The playful
character of the work is due to the fact that even our existence is
conceived of as a game: 'All the world's a stage'—Behan is nearer
to Shakespeare than to Brecht.
    Wolfgang Clemen has written:

> In Shakespeare's last plays, his so-called fairy plays or romances,
> among them *The Tempest, Cymbeline,* and *The Winter's Tale,* we
> find increasingly the impression that reality, in the main, is to
> be understood as appearance; a world of dreams, in which
> fantasy and spells are powerful, begins to supersede reality.[1]

[1] Wolfgang Clemen, *Das Drama Shakespeares, Ausgewählte Vorträge und
Aufsätze* (Gottingen, 1969), p. 129.

Obviously in *The Hostage* there are no dreams or spells, but the presented appearance of life is fantastical and theatrical. Monsewer, with kilt and bagpipe, presents an Irishness larger than life; the two I.R.A. men play the parts of soldiers at war, though one is a teacher and the other a railwayman. One wants to laugh at them, but their playing at warfare leads to a sanguinary end, which, moreover, if forced still further, leads into the realm of fantasy. For the pandemonium which breaks out at the end of the play seems to be a parody of a battle, as if to provide the actors with an opportunity to rage to the full, shooting, shouting and running (p. 105), while Leslie performs a kind of dance before he dies:

> The soldier makes a break for it, zig-zagging across the stage, but every door is blocked. The drum echoes his runs with short rolls. As he makes his last run there is a deafening blast of gun-fire and he drops. (p. 107)

In this world of play-acting everyone is aware that the dead man will rise again in order to sing; everyone knows that he has only pretended to be afraid before he fell; and even then, we all know that soldiers must die, for truth flashes momentarily in appearance. It is in accord with this author's temperament that appearance and reality, or truth, are so closely interwoven.

Behan's biographer called him both 'man and showman', one who played both the Irishman and the rebel, and yet was both. This post was not only forced upon him, it was also closely related to his nature. Again one finds a similarity with Yeats, who, when talking of poets, thought of his nature in the following terms:

> He is Lear, Romeo, Oedipus, Tiresias; he has stepped out of a play . . . He is part of his own phantasmagoria.[1]

Differences apart, in *The Hostage* Behan makes himself part of his own phantasmagoria, for he allows Leslie to describe the author of the play as 'too anti-British', to which the I.R.A. officer replies:

[1] *Essays and Introductions* (1961), p. 509.

Too anti-Irish, you mean. Bejasus, wait till we get him back home. We'll give him what-for for making fun of the Movement.

And Leslie turns to the audience:

He doesn't mind coming over here and taking your money.

Pat explains:

He'd sell his country for a pint. (p. 76)

This kind of irony—which we often call romantic—can be found wherever drama is not considered to be a copy of life, of nature, or of reality, but where a play establishes its own laws. Brendan Behan is working in a long-established tradition, reaching back to the time of the Elizabethan drama.

To what extent Behan was aware of this tradition cannot be ascertained; what is certain, however, is that *The Hostage* could scarcely have been conceived without Shakespeare's example. The common people whom Behan depicts with sympathy, raise their voice with similar power, for the first time, in Shakespeare's history play of *Henry IV*.

In that play the lives of the unimportant merge with the lives of the important. In *The Hostage* Behan has created for himself a part of the Shakespearian cosmos, comparable to that represented in the Dublin-based plays of Sean O'Casey. Politicians and other important persons remain outside this world; they work upon it unseen; but even with Shakespeare there is already a recognition of those who must resign themselves for the present but who will not always do so, since they have their own problems and concerns. As early as Shakespeare (and, as is acknowledged, his work was the first of this kind) comedy and tragedy are intermingled on the stage, leading to brute dissonances; think of the death of Hotspur, followed by the grotesque epilogue of Falstaff,[1] and compare with this the death of the English soldier, where the grave

[1] *I Henry IV*, V. iv.

mourning of the girl is literally outplayed by a wild and gay song. Behan follows in the tracks of Shakespeare. And presumably he would have been a good Elizabethan. The Mermaid tavern would have been as pleasant to him in the way that Leslie found congenial company in the old Dublin house.

VI

Samuel Beckett and the Mass Media

JEAN-JACQUES MAYOUX

FROM his earliest writings—say the poem *Whoroscope* of 1929—Beckett's vision was set and was not to change; simply, the emphasis was to shift from one aspect to the other of a fundamental double-sidedness.

It is by now familiarly admitted—a newspaper article was wittily entitled 'Cogito ergo Sam'—that Beckett is a Cartesian, even if for greater personal intimacy Descartes turns into Geulincx, or if Leibnitz provides, very usefully, the windowless monad ('our windowlessness', says Beckett). He would bully their philosophy a little, if needs be, to make it stress the separateness of man, the fact that since his ancestors have turned to mental life even his body has become a stranger and that he has no true understandable contacts with anything else.

The second point, a corollary, is that whatever contacts he does have are in the form of mechanical stimuli (the body being Descartes's animal-machine), which he himself is tempted, in a sort of absurd emulation, to return to in the form of various aggressions.

A third point may be added: men are tempted to make-believe that they do belong to the external world: they invent human compulsions—family compulsions, class compulsions and metaphysical and religious ones, so as to insert drama into what is a nothingness. If we remember these points we have less difficulty in constructing into coherence the successive works of this imaginative writer, to whom, of course, philosophical data are no more than a support, but an indispensable one.

From the first, if, starting with *Murphy*, we follow all the hints and evidences of shared vision that suggest our seeing Murphy as the central character of all his fiction, Beckett was looking for rest, for peace, for ataraxia; all the agitation—action, love—that we call life, was resisted by this sour 'seedy' solipsist.[1] The first of the Beckettian personae, Belacqua, going back even before *Murphy* to *More Pricks than Kicks* (1934), is one of Dante's sworn brothers to idleness; and so is Murphy, who straps his arms to his armchair in order to achieve perfect motionless contemplation. Starting with these two we see two contrary forces at work, this resolute inertia of the subject on the one hand, and the world's effort to stir the human object into action on the other.

Perhaps this is not the right formulation—rather, there is the need of the subject to be also an object, to be held somehow and tied to some sort of life-drive. Each microcosm invents for himself a macrocosm and starts to receive injunctions from his own images.

If *Murphy* is the first fiction that Beckett completely acknow-ledges, it is not for lack of talent in *More Pricks than Kicks*, but rather because it serves no clear purpose. Murphy, who, the author says, alone of the 'characters' in the book is not a 'puppet' (p. 86), may be taken, in fact, as a richly significant self-symbol. Our seedy solipsist, like Spinoza's God, loves himself with an intellectual love (p. 76). His quest for ataraxia soon turns to a comic, even farcical motive—still strapped to his chair he falls down with it and is only rescued by his mistress from his helpless prostration. He is doomed to disappear into life, and so to be brought back into togetherness becomes the object of a double quest: a quest by others, the forementioned puppets, and a self-quest, that takes him to the lunatic asylum for work as an attendant, for fraternal understanding and for mirror-patterns among the patients, one of whom is significantly named Mr. Endon—the inner one, into whom he seems to be horribly re-absorbed.[2] The quest by others is then a burlesque echo or parody of the self-quest, a pattern to be repeated, later on, in *Molloy*.

The cells at the Magdalen Mental Mercyseat seem to be the first type, as the room of *Endgame* will be the last, of the enclosed

[1] *Murphy* (Calder, 1959), p. 59. (First edition, 1938.)
[2] 'a psychosis so limpid and imperturbable that Murphy felt drawn to it as Narcissus to his fountain.'

monad.¹ They promise blessed seclusion. They deny it because the responsible overseers are sadists who torment the patients, the night through, with sudden, brutal flashings of light. Murphy, who is no sadist, does worse by irresponsibly letting out of his own cell Mr. Endon who blithely takes over the task:

> For quite some little time Mr. Endon had been drifting about the corridors, pressing here a light-switch and there an indicator, in a way that seemed haphazard but was in fact determined by an amental pattern as precise as any of those that governed his chess. Murphy found him in the south transept, gracefully stationed before the hypomanic's pad, ringing the changes on the various ways in which the indicator could be pressed and the light turned on and off. Beginning with the light turned off to begin with he had: lit, indicated, extinguished; lit, extinguished, indicated; indicated, lit, extinguished. Continuing then with the light turned on to begin with he had: extinguished and was seriously thinking of lighting when Murphy stayed his hand. (p. 169)

The violation of the personality which this represents is, like everything in Beckett, symbolical: the quest for quiescence—back to the womb or forth to death—which is typical of all his creatures, is constantly thwarted by persecutions, which may be equated in the beginning to the impact of sensations, and in the end to the pressure of the tribe. Of Murphy's mind, Beckett tells us 'What he called his mind functioned not as an instrument but as a place' (p. 123). This amounts to a statement of utter, but also of necessarily insecure passivity. The place could be invaded, could be turned, possibly could turn itself, perversely, into a ground for the reception of aggressions.

In a less clear-cut manner, the pattern of *Murphy* is repeated in *Molloy*: as Murphy found refuge and shelter from pretentious life-illusions at the Magdalen Mental Mercyseat, so does Molloy seek at least temporary refuge with his Mother or with Lousse (doomed

---

¹ 'the compartment was windowless like a monad ... within the narrow limits of domestic architecture he had never been able to imagine a more creditable representation of (the little world).' (p. 125)

as he is to Ulyssean wanderings), and as Wylie or others seek Murphy, so is Moran sent on a mission to discover Molloy. And here, in Beckett's evolution, comes a decisive difference, not quite prepared by the intervening *Watt*. Watt seems to be free to go to Mr. Knott, although he is not free to stay longer than his appointed time. Moran on the other hand is an 'agent' and is given his orders by a 'messenger'.[1] We are definitely in a Kafkaian world. There is at the source here an invisible master out of all reach, transparently called Youdi, and everywhere an ever mysterious, metamorphic, ruthless 'They'. 'He', 'they', as Moran sees them, as Beckett has invented them for Moran, in fact for himself, are the re-inventions of a cruel God and his tools, an image at least to render account for the dire compulsion to be active. We invent them, however, not only because they do provide such an account, but because we need them to people our utter solitude; and in the course of ages we have reflected this need and repeated these figures in various human figures of similar compulsion, set to work by the collectivity against the individual.

Yet he, they, and their emanations are not even potent to give us a sense of belonging. We remain the unacknowledged, the ignored. Gaber knows where to get hold of Moran and dispose of him, but Moran has not contact or recourse; and as to Vladimir and Estragon, not only can they not get at Godot but even the messenger does not know or recognize them, nor can he identify the one he comes from more definitely than those he comes to. What, if at all, is invented to be self-compelling? The compulsion is there: one would be passive, yet one is active—in the case of one Beckett, creative, even if his protest takes the form of derisive creation, even if the portrait of things which he has been ordered to draw turns to grotesque, monstrous caricature. It is—how frequently the statement is repeated—his doom to write, to make stories: 'my task', 'my pensum'. When will he at last be set free, having satisfied 'them'. He must be sharing in some sort of immemorial guilt and some sort of predestination must then have settled his intolerable fate.

---

[1] 'Here are your instructions, said Gaber; you leave to-day, said Gaber . . . Your son goes with you, said Gaber.' (p. 94)

The awareness of solitude and the desperate need for communication, these then may be the key to all our behaviour. Proust saw his hero as stranded and estranged within his own body. So does Beckett. The grotesque means of communication between Molloy and his mother is a representative symbol of the essence of all such:

> I got into communication with her by knocking on her skull. One knock meant yes, two no, three I don't know, four money, five goodbye. I was hard put to ram this code into her ruined and frantic understanding, but I did it, in the end.[1]

Between human machines communication means compelling stimulation, to act, to respond in some practical manner. The jabs on the buttocks with the tin-opener in *How It Is* are a pretty substitute for those knocks on the skull. In *Act Without Words II*, the long wheel-supported goad which stirs the two characters to 'life' until it is time for their rest is again an obvious variant: the goad might be said to carry persuasive information.

Such is the setting for further developments. Meanwhile it should be stressed that the strong centre of this vision is the condition of the individual, his inexistent existence, his absolute separateness and dereliction, the invention of 'links' with the Outside, the peculiar, the strange 'social contracts' by which he gives the tribe power over himself. All that does make the individual conscious of the tribe and its pressure is somehow imbued with that power; such are the 'mass media', but at the same time the scanty references to them in the early works are invariably derisive. By contrast with the natural inclination of the Beckettian persona to reject activities seen as meaningless, and merely to 'wait' in more or less stoic mood, life as we know it is seen as a series of responses to stimulations almost as mechanical as the light-shocks administered by a lunatic to the lunatics at the Magdalen Mental Mercyseat.

There is in *Murphy* the merest mocking mention of the radio in the trite, trivial language adapted thereto:

[1] *Three Novels* (Calder), p. 18.

'Excellent reception', said Wylie.
'No trace of fading', said Neary ... (p. 149)

in response to Miss Counihan's pompous commonplaces. *Watt* abounds with exchanges in the same vein. Watt meets in the train a large gentleman named Spiro:

> My friends call me Dum, said Mr. Spiro, I am so bright and cheerful.
> D.U.M. Anagram of Mud.
> I edit *Crux*, said Mr. Spiro, the popular catholic monthly ... Our advertisements are extraordinary ... Our prize competitions are very nice ... Of a devout twist they do more good than harm. For example: Rearrange the fifteen letters of the Holy Family to form a question and answer. Winning entry: *Has J. Jurms a po? Yes* ...[1]

Further on we get parodies of the language of commercial advertising. For instance:

> Have you tried Bando, Mr Graves? ... I had tried everything and was thoroughly disgusted when a friend spoke to me of Bando ... I became after four years of Bando, vivacious, restless, a popular nudist, regular in my daily health, almost a father and a lover of boiled potatoes. Bando spelt as pronounced ...[2]

The French version of the thing, turned into literal English, provides in the Essay on Proust:

> I am exhorted not merely to try the aperient of the Shepherd but to try it at 7 o'clock.[3]

'I have to speak,' the victim-hero of *The Unnamable* complains,

[1] *Watt* (Grove Press and Calder, 1959), p. 27. (First edition, Olympia Press, 1953. Written ten years earlier.)
[2] Ibid., p. 170.
[3] *Proust* (Grove Press), p. 6. (First edition, 1931): 'Sept heures, l'heure du Berger'—a now forgotten piece of advertising.

'whatever that means. Having nothing to say, no words but the words of others, I have to speak.' 'The words of others': the words one hears or reads, and that make up, finally, the social person ('I am made of words'), a subject for constant derision. We have encountered in *Watt*, carefully flattened for us to recognize it the better, the pseudo-language of the Press, that Joyce had introduced us to in the same spirit, in the 'Eolus' episode of *Ulysses*, set at the offices and printing-works of the *Telegraph*. We meet it again in *Happy Days* as Winnie slowly spells out, to pass the time, the words printed on her toothbrush: 'Fully guaranteed genuine pure hog's setae'. Willie having retained from the days when they both functioned in the midst of life-illusions, some newspaper fragment, seems to derive a relish from its futilities: 'His Grace and Most Reverend father in God Dr. Carolus Hunter dead in tub.'[1] The paper may be ten years old. By now its desolate clichés are immemorial: 'Opening for smart youth' . . . 'Wanted bright boy'. The 'filthy postcard' that is Willie's next solace is another way to spell out, to distribute, to sell, the words of the tribe.

By way of contrast with the simple and absolute dereliction of Vladimir, Estragon, Hamm or Clov, *Happy Days* introduces a new element, the same, in another form, that we have already pointed out in *Act Without Words II*: the external stimulation, the goad without which there is no conceivable reason why one should go through the formalities of living on, day after day. Willie and Winnie may seem utterly forgotten, but the bell sees to it that they wake up properly and prepare for another 'happy day', then, that they, at the proper time, enjoy their allotted rest.

The foregoing pages have had for their main intent and purpose to show in what network of attitudes, thoughts and representations, an ambiguous interest in various mass-media was going to be born and to develop.

It became specific, precise, technical, for the first time, I think, when in 1956–7 he wrote *All That Fall*, commissioned as a radio play for the B.B.C. Beckett's ingenious and intensely technical

---

[1] *Happy Days* (Grove Press, 1961), p. 15.

mind became absorbed in the problems of this peculiar mode of representation, the ways and means of conveying a certain vision through the ear alone; and out of the absorption a revelation came to him: this was a language precisely fitted to his needs. Through the senses we build our world representation, or illusion: Beckett we have seen as closer to Berkeley than to Descartes because Berkeley takes great trouble absolutely to separate us from external reality; and he does it through a close investigation of the working of the senses in perception. It provides a purely phenomenal world, a ghost of a world, which becomes the ghostlier if one of the main senses, the sight for instance, be somehow suppressed, bringing about practically a reduction of perception to another main sense: hearing. Hence the fascination for Beckett of making scenes for radio which create such a reduction to the audible. In *All That Fall* the first noun, and the second word, is *sounds*; arrangements of sounds, severally, then together, follow. Mrs. Rooney is perceived, is known, through the sound of her dragging feet; all is identified by insignificant sound turned significant; while a visible landscape would remain separate, external, something we pass through without being *modified*, sounds here become the web on which our thoughts are hung. Perhaps merely the new, the unusual angle on 'reality' is in question: the imagination is more decisively brought into play because all those of us who are not blind are accustomed to build their reality as a sequence of sights rather than as a sequence of sounds. Here the sound of a thing is its very definition, as shown by Beckett's directions:

> the wind—brief wind
> the birds—brief chirp
> the cows—brief moo
> the sheep—brief baa[1]

Distinct sounds, connected sounds, words as sounds and arrangements of words are not the material texture only but the very substance of the play. A purely audible caricature such as is

[1] *All That Fall* (Faber, 1957), p. 29.

created by the 'sound of efforts' when the enormous Mrs. Rooney is pushed into the car then extracted from it seems to be disproportionately effective for its simple means. If sounds seem to run away in happy new-won freedom, words are the most strangely freed of all. A word will suddenly loom powerfully as if endowed with a power of revelation: 'Oh to be in atoms, in atoms!' Mrs. Rooney exclaims in sudden despair: '(Frenziedly) ATOMS!' (p. 12). Words choose their affinities through tempting associations rather than sense: Mr. Rooney thus enumerates the horrors of home life: 'scrubbing, waxing, *waning* . . .' (p. 31); or Mr. Tyler ruthfully declares: 'We are doubly late, trebly, *quadrupedly* late . . .' (p. 11).

Sounds are brought into play both in their precision and their ambiguity, in their denotation and connotation, to conjure a vivid if elusive presence, slightly oneiric, in which objects are insistent and abolished by turns: on the road to the station, then in the station, the dragging and shuffling of heavy feet, the bicycle and its bursting tyre, the old car that won't start then starts with a vengeance—which vengeance falls on the cackling hen.

Objects merely named, not nailed down to the clearness of sight, may have no final identity, only a sort of intention, conveying a symbol. They are rather key-words to some mysterious lock: such is the almost central motive of the ball which falls from Mr. Rooney's pocket: 'it looks like a kind of ball. And yet it it is not certainly a ball.' If it is a ball, perhaps it has been unchilded; perhaps a child has been unballed; certainly a child has died under the wheels of the train. In this world of sounds no clear connecting lines can be traced but obscure systems of waves seem to intersect.[1]

'My view of life,' Molloy muses, 'has been exaggeratedly formal.' Beckett's became increasingly so. One might term him an innate structuralist, or at least a formalist, for whom—as in any case no so-called reality is to be taken at its face-value—the creative writer

[1] The ball theme is supplemented by a musical theme: radio into radio sounds of *Death and the Maiden*.

has no call to imitate it and give us a set of second degree illusions. Beckett thus plays with his data, which come to him, surge before him, as from a sort of day-dream or reverie, his task as an artist being to arrange, to dispose them; not unaware that any such arrangement is arbitrary, he has set himself at a distance of unconcern. It seems to me an aberration to denounce *How It Is* as a decomposition, a disintegration of language. It is marked by the invention of the rough and ready language that is needed not to 'ape' life but adequately to express a by now total disbelief in the meaning of it or anything in it, particularly of the so-called human relations, now reduced from the comparative complexity of *Malone* or *Godot* to disconcertingly simple alternations of schemes or patterns. The narrator muses on possibilities that might in the end lead him from wax recordings to experiment with computers: 'a whole life, generations, or else ebonite recordings or similar, you can imagine it, nothing prevents, *mix up change the natural order play with that.*'

Apart from the hasty plural, 'generations', this is precisely what Beckett was to do next in *Krapp's Last Tape* (1958), having found with his instinctively keen interest in techniques that what the record could not do for him the tape-recorder would do perfectly, with the shufflings, the flashbacks in immediate confrontation with the present, that he sought. Alan Schneider in his comments on *Film*[1] which we shall examine later, notes: 'It was Sam who had written a play mastering the definitive use of a tape-recorder even though he had never owned one.'

Here again, although Krapp is visible to us,[2] what counts is that the past instead of being represented, let us say by a written journal, is heard as a living voice, although it is only by a sort of courtesy that we can consider the man who owned it still to be alive, he himself being savagely aware of his total change. At a distance alternately of detached curiosity or seething fury, he listens to his plans, his self-appreciations, his moments of intermittent, uncertain emotion on decisive occasions. The depth-

[1] *Film* (Grove Press, 1969), p. 65.
[2] Let us note, by the way, that in recent productions of *Krapp* Beckett seems to have been much less insistent on visible grotesqueness—size of shoes, etc.

dimension is singularly vivid and expresses through retrospect the complete futility of what has been the living moment. The play reflects the externalized persistence of the dead self that believes in life, rejected by the present man with life itself.

Embers (1959), again a moving and admirable radio piece, goes in appearance to the opposite. It is the pressure of the obsessed mind that is exerted on the blankness of surrounding 'reality' and turns it into a series of vehement hallucinations, vividly present for us as successive sounds, noises, shouts of the persecuting masters, wails of the persecuted child:

> Hooves! (*Pause. Louder.*) Hooves! (*Sound of hooves walking on hard road.*) Again![1] . . . Close your eyes and listen to it, what would you think it was? . . . A drip! A drip! (*Sound of drip.*) Again! . . . No! (*Drip cut off.*)[2]

The mind now, under whatever compulsion it may act, creates his own reality, with whatever distortions his subjective condition may command. The radio effects of amplification remind us of the expressionist cinema. The hammered note of music 'Eff!' and Addie's wail are amplified to paroxysm.

Embers has a setting that obviously haunts Beckett's imagination before it does ours—again a purely audible setting, of the noise of Henry's boots in the shingle, and the sea dully breaking, a sort of natural voice across which his vehemence clamours for the voices that are the motives of his neurosis. Ada the wife, Addi the child, are brought in, Ada for the routine dialogue of yesteryears, Addie for the intolerable horror of an upbringing fiercely to be rejected.

A simple case for us to observe and study, *Embers* will help us understand *Cascando* or *Words and Music* (1962), two more radio plays, the one French and the other English, two sophisticated variations on the theme or vision of a more and more decisively split personality creating its own world, bringing into it, to populate it, the required pseudo-characters, instituting the

[1] *Embers*, with *Krapp's Last Tape* (Faber, 1959), pp. 21–2.
[2] p. 24.

dialogues, carrying on the conflicts and dramas of a mental micro-cosm running down. Within the one, invisible, unreal body, a structural arrangement of multiple and separate, however depend-ent, parts, has taken the place of the single person. In *Words and Music* Words, an automaton like Lucky pretending to thinking powers, is found at the beginning occupying the scene with another inmate, Music. Words complains of this association as of a compulsion: 'How much longer pent up here in the dark? With *you*!'[1] Ignoring this detested partner, Words rehearses and brings out in a void his composition, a sort of empty Aristotelian school-boy piece: 'Theme:... Sloth (*Pause. Rattled off, low.*) Sloth is of all the passions ...' He does it—did we say 'in a void'?—rather in hating conflict with Music who tries to put in his ever-soothing bit of pleasant accommodating sound. Croak, the third person in this Trinity, assuming uneasy authority, but not very capable of Pozzo-like assertiveness, although termed 'My Lord', clearly needs both partners, Words whom he calls Joe and Music whom he calls Bob, and tries to bring them to team together. He at once re-starts Joe, as if capable not only of 'thinking' but of awareness, on a new theme: not Sloth but Love. Words is not to be deflected by such a paltry matter as a change of 'theme' and at once starts: 'Love is of all the passions ...', and the rest of it follows unaltered, except that when absent-mindedly he comes to say 'Sloth is the ...' he quickly catches himself up to resume 'LOVE is the ...' (p. 28), until Croak, with a 'violent thump of club' appeals to Music or 'Bob' for a change in spite of the protests of Joe, who seems now, perhaps in defence of his anti-musical, ironical function, to wake up to some kind of awareness of substance to be joined to words, and turns to questioning: 'Is Love the word?... Is Soul the word?... Do we mean love when we say love? ... soul, when we say soul?' (p. 29), till Croak appeals to 'Bob' and obtains 'Love and soul music' instead of dis-quieting words then changes the theme again to 'Age', extracting now nothing from Joe but confused mumblings, and finally trying to bring his microcosm back to unity with a violent thump: 'Together, dogs!' (p. 30), so that Joe has to try and sing the words

[1] *Words and Music* (Faber, 1962): edition with *Play* (Faber, 1964), p. 27.

of his theme to music, while Music (Bob) with superior patience plays through alone, then, with an opening, invites Words to join, pauses, invites again and finally *accompanies* very softly. Croak, being unhappily haunted by a face which Words tries to define for him, bringing an anguished 'Lily!' to his lips, has begged in vain 'My Comforts! Be friends!' and departs unsatisfied.

What have we been listening to? Something, it seems to me that harks back to the tradition of the medieval morality, a drama without reference to external reality, an episode in the adventures of the split mind: so, very modern.

Another such episode, and a confirmation of this very singular vision, is to be found in *Cascando*, written for the French radio. Again here we get the myth of the cruel compeller (Opener) and the reluctantly compelled (Voice), with again Music at the service of Opener. The split is emphasized: 'They say, "It's in his head." No, I open . . . so, at will. It's my life, I live on that' (p. 42). He takes us to witness when 'opening' to music: 'And that . . . is that mine too', as if obviously music could *not* be properly his own (p. 46). 'I open both,' he has previously stated—both Voice and Music—adding, 'from one world to another it's as though they drew together' (p. 44).

The compeller, in fact, is compelled, is only the intermediary, truly the porter of the mind, letting in all the fictions and dreams, all the 'stories', that press from the outside into its emptiness. Murphy's mind, we must now recall, was 'a place'

> I'm afraid to open.
> But I must open.
> So I open.

A tormented self, or rather part-self, struggles against a compulsion which seems external, and is irresistible at the same time as it is unbearable. The individual, or his inmost core of negative authenticity, experiences nothing but a will to passivity, wants nothing but quiet, peace, a folding back against his silence; but it is ceaselessly harried by a superego truly perceived as an oppressive stranger.

Thus situated, the person bursts into fragments of furious incoherence, passing by turns from guilty defiance to guilty abjection, and thwarted in all its efforts to escape, to find a refuge, by quasi-galvanic stimulations. When Beckett did *Eh Joe*[1] for British television, he must again have found in the joint work of the camera and the spotlights, both converging on a tormented face, a curious coincidence with his own vision. Joe is at bay. His accumulated guilts seek and search him while he is trying to lock them out of the room where we find him, closing doors or cupboards with futile keys, pulling curtains, peering under bed (pp. 15–16). It is first his terrified back that we encounter, a back that senses unbearable presences and conveys this more intensely than the front might. The camera guided as ever, by Beckett's careful, precise, detailed directions, follows Joe about, full length, at a distance that remains unchanged. Then it properly sets to work, advancing by cruel, relentless degrees towards a nearer and nearer close-up of the face until the Voice stops it, as if it had been pinned down sufficiently, unable now to escape listening:

> After this opening pursuit, between first and final close-up of face, camera has nine slight moves in towards face, say four inches each time. Each move is stopped by voice resuming, never camera move and voice together. This would give position of camera when dolly stopped by first word of text as one yard from maximum close-up of face. Camera does not move between paragraphs till clear that pause (say three seconds) longer than between phrases. Then four inches in say four seconds when movement stopped by voice resuming. (p. 15)

All this, minutely stipulated by Beckett, might be the programme of ingenious torture in some vision of 'darkness at noon'. Voice and searching light induce a terror of being held, seen, revealed. 'Not afraid a bug might see you?' All that has been given him, without his ever making any return (Beckett is a moralist), bringing him finally to this, to this only obsession, 'kill your dead in your head'.

Play is a play, no mass media being involved, but it is very near in

[1] *Eh Joe* (Faber, 1967). (First performance, 1966.)

its conception to a television piece. The three inurned characters are 'dead' in the sense at any rate of being all past: when and how does 'death' really intervene in the Beckettian universe? It is here seen, all passion spent, as a sort of catalepsy, in which the three might be left to everlasting quiet. But the compulsion scheme is again at work. The dead are galvanized into rehearsing indefinitely the paltry capital scenes of their cheap triangular pattern. What they say is mere commonplace, yet we are held by what is much more than showmanship, again Beckett's vision of persecution and compulsion. Even in death the harried conscience, it would seem, cannot escape our, by now, familiar proddings and stimuli. 'Their speech is provoked by a spotlight projected on faces alone ... The transfer of light from one face to another is immediate.'[1] It is significant that the first text of Beckett's key stage-direction after this was 'the response to light is *not quite* immediate', and that '*not quite*' was then crossed out: he has suppressed a delay which at first must have appeared meaningful.

The pattern of stimulus and response seems to emphasize the heterogeneity of two elements, but we know how fundamental the ambiguity of the process and what it involves must remain. As these dead are still in some way living consciences, so the spotlight, dramatically external as it appears throughout, is yet a sudden mode of self-awareness translated into more or less metaphysical terms.

W1 asks: 'Is anyone looking at me?' (p. 17)—M. will ask in the end: 'Am I as much as ... being seen?' (p. 22). Yet when the spot hit him just previously he had said: 'And now that you are ... mere eye ... just looking. At my face. On and off ...' 'Looking for something. In my face. Some truth. In my eyes ... Mere eye. No mind. *Opening and shutting on me*' (p. 21).

'A unique inquisitor' Beckett termed the light in his own note. If we should doubt that in the end the searching spotlight will have to be returned to its source in the concerned self, *Film*[2] will help us make up our minds.

[1] *Play* (Faber, 1968), p. 21.
[2] *Film* (Grove Press, 1969): Beckett's scenario, with an essay by Alan Schneider on producing *Film*.

The scenario for this extraordinary venture of Beckett's into the cinema proper, dated 1963, the trip to New York for the making of it, and Alan Schneider's journal of the day-to-day problems of the production, including Beckett's connection with Buster Keaton, do not throw bright light only on that single work, but also on the larger meanings of Beckett's creation in those years.

He begins his script with a general philosophical proposition which is not, as it happens, *Cogito ergo sum*, but *Esse est percipi* (p. 11): in the angle between the two formulas resides a definite and important shift, opening a way to mass media. The 'mass medium' immediately involved here, *id est* the camera-work, gives the individual the sense of being got at, both perceived and reflected so that he seeks the refuge of 'non-being in flight from extraneous perception breaking down in inescapability of self-perception'; such are the words of Beckett's own analysis, barely tempered by his characteristic qualification, 'no truth-value attaches to the above', since nothing is true anyway, and clinched by his final remark 'that the pursuing perceiver is the self': understand, the consciousness of personal identity.

The person under cruel observation in *Film* is split between his bodily presence, everywhere denoted O, or Object, and the observing camera, an external projection of this consciousness, termed E or Eye. The camera angle, shown in a series of careful diagrams in Beckett's scenario, becomes expressive of the relation between E and O, of O's sense of being seen, or not, of his chance of retaining 'immunity': the author's geometrical visualization is so precise that he has set the angle at the shift from 45 to 46 degrees. When conscious of being perceived, O reacts, for instance, by halting and cringing towards a wall. The camera-eye becomes what we might term a central and symbolic eye in the room-setting. The consciousness of being seen includes the dog, the cat, the mirror, the window, the parrot, the goldfish, the print of God the Father with a severe stare, even the accidentally eye-like perforations at the top of the rocking-chair: for Beckett is quick to be struck by converging accidents.[1]

[1] 'The rocker we were using happened to have two holes in the headrest which began to glare at us.' Alan Schneider, p. 85.

Joe-like, 'O' (Buster Keaton in the film) draws the curtains, covers the mirror with a rug and the parrot-cage with his coat, puts out dog and cat. Then he sets out to destroy his photographs, the eyes of the past as they might be termed, contained in a folder which opens and shuts by tying together two eyelets, 'another pair of eyes' for O to avoid. (*Ibid.*)

The eye-motive in the initial conception was to be present from the beginning, the intention being to 'open with a huge menacing close-up of an eye held as long as possible and then opening to reveal the pupil searching and then focussing' (p. 85).

Beckett knows admirably what he wants of the camera, and also he is quite aware of the technical difficulty of securing it; perhaps the only point he misses is that the spectator will not have time enough, nor perhaps enough ready critical acumen, to get the benefit of oversubtle intentions. For the camera has all along to play two different parts. It is the malevolent E or Eye focussed on O, the rest of what it perceives being marginal; but it is also the instrument of O's perception of environment, uncertain, ever blurred, as for instance in his view of the print of God the Father. Alan Schneider notes that, co-operative as Beckett was, there could be no compromise with his vision which was 'completely dominant', nor with 'the audacity of his concepts'—'a highly disciplined use of two specific camera viewpoints'. 'What was required was not merely a subjective camera and an objective camera but actually two different "visions" of reality' (p. 65). The professional man is seen to be subjugated by this most unorthodox user, and concedes also 'that Beckett had not lost his mind in confining those camera angles so rigidly to 45 to 46 degrees' (p. 68). 'We shot,' he notes, 'more 180 degrees and 360 degrees pans than in a dozen westerns.'[1]

The example of *Film* is in my judgement vividly instructive, and we may with it bring this essay to a conclusion. For it is probably by now a glimpse of the obvious that Beckett has created a fantastic world out of the decomposition of the once secure personality; but what we have tried to show is that he

[1] It should be stressed, of course, that this being a play on Beckett's theory of vision, the film is silent.

became by degrees aware of the part that an intelligent use of various mass media, radio, television, cinema, and their means and instruments, sounds, lights, images, could play in selecting and splitting various aspects of conscious awareness, as well as recalling how they provide effective techniques of pressure and aggression against it. They gave Beckett irreplaceable elements of purely concrete language (Music as the unmixed presence of music and so on) to play with and use in his dramatizations. The mass media used (perhaps abused) in a manner that it would have been difficult to foresee and harnessed to a near-solipsist vision have finally, if I am right, brought no mean contribution to the invention of a singular world.

VII

Language and Laughter

GLORIA CIGMAN

J. Do you know Margaret B——?
R. Yes. She's minute.
G. I didn't know you had a newt.

WE like to make each other laugh. Sometimes we tell anecdotes and sometimes we have sudden insights into possibilities in language. Those who spot these possibilities swiftly enough, exploit them skilfully enough and provoke laughter enough are called witty. This thought and my subsequent exploration of the relationship between language and humour were triggered off by the above snippet of breakfast-table conversation. I set about collecting as many examples as I could find of as many kinds of linguistic humour as I could recognize.

I concentrated on modern usage because here we can draw on more certain knowledge of semantic intention; a certainty which diminishes as we go further back in time. For example, can we know whether the following passages from Chaucer are examples of humour?

> She cold was, and withouten sentement,
> For aught he woot, for breth ne felt he non;
> And this was him a pregnant argument
> That she was forth out of this world agon.[1]

and [Criseyde speaking]:

> I am a womman, as ful wel ye woot . . .[2]

---

[1] *Troilus and Criseyde*, iv. 1177 ff.
[2] *Troilus and Criseyde*, iv. 1261.

They seem funny to me, but the first passage is almost certainly not meant to be.

My central concern has been to look at how language is operative in humour. I avoided such inviting abstractions as the nature of humour itself and the Englishness of English humour, but gave some thought to the more tangible question of medium of transmission. The oral transmission of radio humour and the visual transmission of humour immobilized on the printed page clearly relate significantly to the nature of the language generated in each. Compare the rapidity of Goon humour, on the one hand, and the studied complexity of Ogden Nash on the other.

The result of my survey was the formulation of categories and kinds, and a structure to contain both. These are set out in the simplified tables below.

	Mode of expression			Mode of thought
Syntax	Sentence Structure Idiom Word order	Dis-collocation		Cliché-splitting Cliché-coining Use and abuse of collocation Jargon
Words	Word formation Split compounds Anomaly			
Trans-mission	Metanalysis Rhyme manipulation Distortion of sound Visual distortion Metre Homophony	Ambiguity		Total separation of meanings Functional change Semantic nuance Puns
		Precision		Illogical usage satirized Abstract/concrete Relation of word to referent

This structure is tentative. The categories are not as self-contained as the tables suggest because so many features of linguistic humour spill over into each other. As the tables indicate, my basis for the discussion which follows is the notion that linguistic humour is generated in two ways: by mode of expression, or by mode of thought. Each must, of course, embody the other, but this exploration assumes that sometimes the one is dominant and sometimes the other.

As a starting point, I suggest that the categories which I have classified under the headings *Syntax, Words,* and *Transmission* demonstrate humour imposed by the mode of expression, and those which are headed *Discollocation, Ambiguity,* and *Precision* demonstrate a humorous mode of thought imposed upon language. I will illustrate these proposed polarities.

When Ogden Nash gives a poem the title 'Bankers are just like anybody else, except richer',[1] humour is imposed on the basic statement that bankers are richer than anybody else by an abuse of the expectation arising from the syntax. The apparent incongruity of the correlatives 'just like ... except' can be and often is righted by an assumption that a comparison of degree is being expressed, rather than a difference of quality. Thus, if I say 'John is just like his brother, except friendlier', I am sustaining the notion of just-likeness by implying that both brothers are friendly—only barely sustaining it, perhaps, but the construction puts the idea of resemblance first, then follows with a comparative. A different construction would be needed to express total contrast. The statement is not that John's brother is unfriendly, but that he is less friendly. But the humour of Ogden Nash's statement lies in his shattering of all notions of just-likeness by picking out a feature of bankers which is far from being common to everybody ('just like anybody else'), i.e. having a lot of money. He uses a comparative adjective where the assumptions of resemblance which underlie comparison cannot be made. Humour is achieved by a deliberate violation of the logic suggested by the syntax.

In contrast, the humour of the following example, from Thurber's *The 13 Clocks,* arises from the mode of thought, i.e. from the semantics and not the mechanics of the language:

> He showed his lower teeth. 'We all have flaws,'
> he said, 'and mine is being wicked.'[2]

[1] Ogden Nash, *The Face is Familiar* (London, 1954), p. 7.
[2] James Thurber, *The 13 Clocks and The Wonderful O* (London, 1966), p. 70.

The idea of a flaw is too small to encompass a defect of the magnitude of 'being wicked'. A similar disparity, this time involving the word 'fault', contributes to the rather laboured irony of these sayings, recorded by Tilley:[1]

He has but one fault, he is nought.

And, somewhat modified:

Your main fault is you are good for nothing.

Here it is impossible to bridge the semantic gap. It would seem to count for little that something is a man's only, or main, fault, if it is of such magnitude that no virtue could possibly compensate. What could redeem a man from being 'nought' or 'good for nothing'?

I shall now discuss some of the categories and kinds in the tables.

Syntax and word order

In the example from Ogden Nash already discussed, the humour-determining factor was syntax. Jane Austen manipulates syntax effectively for humorous-satirical ends:

Her father was a clergyman, without being neglected or poor, and a very respectable man, though his name was Richard and he had never been handsome.[2]

We are being prepared, at the onset of *Northanger Abbey*, for the ensuing gentle debunking of a whole set of false assumptions. The apposition phrase ('without, etc. . . .') rejects the popular image of the neglected and poor clergyman by pretending to accept it. The particle 'though' leads the reader to anticipate a denial of some expectation aroused by the idea of respectability:

[1] M. P. Tilley, *A Dictionary of Proverbs in England in the Seventeenth and Eighteenth Centuries* (Ann Arbor, 1950), Entry F108, p. 205.
[2] Jane Austen, *Northanger Abbey* (Zodiac Press, 1962), p. 9.

some imagined association between respectability and being called
Richard, or respectability and being handsome. In fact, these three
pieces of information are quite independent of each other. Eventually the heroine is to learn that most of her assumptions and
expectations are similarly unfounded in reality.

In the following passage, from Thurber's *The Wonderful O*,
humour is achieved by patterning of words and syntax: regular
repetition of the verb 'lost', and an accumulation of parallel clauses
linked by identical syntax and a succession of indefinite quantita-
tive adjectives:

> some lads lost their lasses, and most men lost their tempers, and
> all men lost their patience, and a few men lost their minds.[1]

Within this orderly structure, however, Thurber's phrases are far
from parallel. The loss of lasses is rendered light-hearted by the
jingling of the alliteration and the folksy 'lads/lasses' collocation;
the loss of tempers and patience is of middle weight in the
scale of afflictions; but 'a few men lost their minds' is set apart by
its gravity, and by the sudden drop to 'few' after the mounting
from 'some' to 'most' to 'all'. Ultimately, the passage is funny
because of the absurdity of the situation which is incompatible
with tragedy.[2]

A quite different manipulation of syntax is found when Ogden
Nash paraphrases idiomatic collocations and weaves the resultant
distortion into the syntax of his verse, as in this poem about people
who get things done:

> They have budgets and what is more they live inside of them,
> Even though it means eating things made by recipes clipped
> from the Sunday paper that you'd think they would have died
> of them.[3]

The basic collocation there is 'to live within a budget'. The meaning is held in place by the stable and straightforward syntax of the

[1] Op. cit., p. 116.
[2] See pp. 113–14 below.
[3] Op. cit., 'A Stitch too Late is my Fate', p. 23.

first stentence, and the humour is intensified by the ensuing sentence in which the collocation 'to die of eating something' is embodied in an elaborate piece of syntactical eccentricity. Conventional syntax, given the same words, would have thrown out the pronoun 'them' and arrived at the following structure:

> Even though it means eating things of which you'd think they would have died made by recipes clipped from the Sunday papers.

Ogden Nash achieves a variety of humorous effects through departures from orthodox word order:

> Now curfew tolls in the old church steeple,
> Bidding good night to sensible people;
> Now thousands and thousands of people sensible
> Think staying up later is reprehensible;
> . . . .
> Now owls desist from to-wit-to-wooing,
> And ne'er-do-wells from their ne'er-well-doing;[1]

Here changes of word order contribute to rhyme, to word formation, and to functional change. It may be that the conversion of the onomatopoeic phrase 'to-wit-to-woo' to a verbal noun generated the change of word order on the next line, or that the 'ne'er-well-doing' word order change generated both its own conversion and the preceding verbal phrase 'to desist from to-wit-to-wooing'. Either way, the mode of expression is the primary factor in determining the humour.

Words

An exploration of the uses of individual words revealed a number of different devices. Ogden Nash expresses antithesis or contrast by nonce uses of selected morphemes,[2] sometimes in new formations:

---

[1] Op. cit., 'Read this Vibrant Exposé', p. 34.

[2] Morphemes are the minimal units of sense of which words may be composed. Free morphemes can exist as separate words; bound morphemes can only occur as parts of words, e.g. in the word *unfriendly*, *un* and *ly* are bound morphemes, *friend* is a free morpheme.

There are two kinds of people who blow through life like a breeze.
And one kind is gossipers, and the other kind is gossipees.[1]

and sometimes by freeing morphemes which are usually bound and almost—but not quite—giving them the status of separate words, as in:

So far as I know, mankind is the only section of creation
That is doomed to either pers- or ex-piration.[2]

Thurber achieves the conversion of parts to whole words more successfully in:

'Weep for me, maiden,' said the King, 'for I am ludicrous and laughable, with my foot caught in this trap. I am no longer ert, for I have lost my ertia.'[3]

As with his deviations from normal word order, Ogden Nash uses new word formations to achieve rhymes:

... when it comes to physical prowess,
Why woman is a wow, or should I say a wowess?[4]

... in celestial circles all the run-of-the-mill angels would rather be archangels or at least cherubim and seraphim,
And in the legal world all the little process-servers hope to grow up into great big bailiffim and sheriffim.[5]

Another kind of word formation isolates units (not always morphemes) of di- or polysyllabic words. The Goons exploit hidden homophony:

[1] Op. cit., 'I Have it on Good Authority', p. 11.
[2] Op. cit., ' Grasshoppers are very Intelligent', p. 86.
[3] *The 13 Clocks*, p. 41.
[4] Op. cit., 'Oh, Please don't Get Up!', p. 113.
[5] Op. cit., 'Kindly Unhitch that Star, Buddy', p. 110.

H

This will earn me a fortune, if not a five-tune, or a six-tune, or a seven-tune.*

And, in reply to a man who wants to buy a penguin:

'I'll just look in this catalogue.'
'I don't want a cat; I want a penguin. Look in the penguin-logue.'*

Both the Goons and Thurber create humour through the splitting of compound words:

Eccles: Forsooth, sooth, sooth, sooth, sooth . . .
Traveller: What manner of idiot is this that keeps saying 'sooth'?
Eccles: (Aside) Little does he know that I'm a soothsayer.*

And, from Thurber, a limerick:

> There was an old coddle so molly,
> He talked in a glot that was poly,
> His gaws were so gew
> That his laps became dew,
> And he ate only pops that were lolly.[1]

The underlying logic of those two examples is very different. That of the Goons is akin to the preoccupation with exactitude discussed below, under the heading *Precision.* The vocation of a soothsayer could, logically, be to say 'sooth'—just as a town-crier *could* be one who cries 'town'. It just doesn't happen to be so. But Thurber's compound-splitting works differently. It pretends that the divided parts of words are viable morphemes and, moreover, that we know what they all mean. Not dissimilar is Ogden Nash's device of creating new compounds by analogy: 'heehaw/shehaw', 'jackass/jennyass' and 'the miserable town where the girls were too boisterous and the boys were too girlsterous'.[2]

* All quotations with an asterisk are from *The Goon Show,* broadcast on B.B.C. Radio between 1952 and 1960.
[1] *The 13 Clocks,* p. 52.
[2] Op. cit., 'Who Understands Who Anyhow?', p. 168.

A final example of humour depending on the nature of words—as distinct from their sense—is found in the following anonymous poem:

> I said, 'This horse, sir, will you shoe?'
> And soon the horse was shod.
> I said, 'This deed, sir, will you do?'
> And soon the deed was dod!
>
> I said, 'This stick, sir, will you break?'
> At once the stick he broke.
> I said, 'This coat, sir, will you make?'
> And soon the coat he moke![1]

Here an apparent anomaly of English preterite formation is parodied in the creation of preterites by the kind of logical analogy that has often been observed in the language of small children, e.g. 'I am nice, amn't I?', which is perhaps quaint rather than funny, and 'Don't argue!', 'Don't arg *me*' which is an amusing, if puzzling, example of confusion arising from homophony. It is akin to the Goons' 'fortune/five-tune', but more complex because the reinterpreted parts of the word (from 'argue' to 'arg you', or 'arg, you') involve a change in word function and, therefore, in sentence structure. I recently heard of another example of complex word formation by analogy in a primary school classroom. A child was trying to thread a needle:

Teacher: What are you doing?
Child: I'm seefing it.
Teacher: You're *what*?
Child: I'm seefing it'll go through.

Sight and sound
My third category of humour determined by rather than determining linguistic method is entirely dependent upon the mode of transmission: the sight *or* sound of language.

The first of these is metanalysis: a re-arrangement of words, or parts of words, so as to change the combination but not the

---

[1] J. M. Cohen, *The Penguin Book of Comic and Curious Verse* (1952), p. 221.

sequence of morphemes and phonemes (sounds) in adjacent words. The device is predominantly visual in Ogden Nash:

> Spring is what winter
> Always gazinta.[1]

> ... he went and tried to borrow some money from Ferdinand
> But Ferdinand said America was a bird in the bush and he'd
> rather have a berdinand.[2]

> There is a phase of life that I have never heard discussed in any
> seminar,
> And that is that all women think men are funny and all men
> think that weminar.[3]

The Goons, on the other hand, using an entirely non-visual medium, use entirely non-visual metanalysis:

> And so they forged ahead. They also forged legs, teeth and
> knees.*

and:

> 'Admit it! You're a spy!'
> 'I'm not a spy. I'm a shepherd.'
> 'Aha! Shepherd's pie!'*

Akin to this method is the minor distortion of sound sometimes introduced to force existing words to fit a rhyme pattern. Again, Ogden Nash provides examples:

> I would live all my life in nonchalance and insouciance
> Were it not for making a living, which is rather a nouciance.[4]

[1] Op. cit., 'The Passionate Pilgrim and the Dispassionate Public: The Tragedy of the Machine Age', p. 16.
[2] Op. cit., 'Columbus', p. 39.
[3] Op. cit., 'Who Understands Who Anyhow?' p. 167.
[4] Op. cit., 'Introspective Reflection', p. 12.

You go to Paris and live on champagne, wine and cognac
If you're a dipsomognac.[1]

Less often, but with the same end in view, he forces foreign words
into Anglicized—or Americanized—pronunciation. It can be
seen that this would be very much less successful transmitted orally
because the hearer might not immediately understand the words
and would miss what follows while puzzling over them:

... if mink is no better than *lapin* to you
Why you don't even deserve to have anything nice and exciting
happen to you.[2]

and, on bathers versus showerers:

... from the way people *lave* themselves
You can tell how under other circumstances they will *behave*
themselves.[3]

Another kind of oral distortion brings about a major shift of sense
by means of a minor shift in sound. The Goons speak of a political
statement by the 'Prime Monster'. Lewis Carroll's amphibians
learn 'Reeling and Writhing . . . Mystery, ancient and modern,
with Seaography'.[4]

I have never been sure whether it was all right, i.e. sound of
literary judgement, to be amused by the short measure and reiterated rhymes of Skelton.[5] But no such doubts arise in these metric-
ally similar modern examples:

[1] Op. cit., 'Oh to be Odd!' p. 117.
[2] Op. cit., 'The Anatomy of Happiness', p. 136.
[3] Op. cit., 'Splash!' p. 122.
[4] *Alice's Adventures in Wonderland*, p. 129. All references to *Alice* are to M.
Gardner's *The Annotated Alice* (London, 1960).
[5] O *cat of carlish kind,*
  The fiend was in thy mind
  When thou my bird untwined [destroyed]
  I would thou hadst been blind!
Taken from 'Philip Sparrow' in *The Complete Poems of John Skelton*, ed. P.
Henderson (London, 1959), p. 68. The poem is, of course, part satire, part
parody. Even so, I suspect that some of our mirth is misdirected and somewhat
patronizing.

Are you sure it is a hat?
And if so, what was the matter
With the hatter?

. . . .

Is its aspect, rear and frontal
Intended to disgruntle?
Or was it accidental
And is he now repental?[1]

and:

In spite of her sniffle
Isabel's chiffle.
Some girls with a sniffle
Would be weepy and tiffle.

. . . .

But when Isabel's snivelly
She's snivelly civilly.[2]

The following piece of Goon dialogue is an example of humour which can only be transmitted through our experience of sound:

Q. How do you spell 'penguin'?
A. P. N. Gywnn.
Q. How do you pronounce it?
A. P.E.N.G.U.I.N.*

When we encounter that on the printed page we have to carry out a mental reading-aloud to grasp the point. This is true of all humour depending on homophony. Much of Lewis Carroll's humour comes into this category—which is, after all, quite consistent with his ostensible purpose of telling a story aloud to a child:

We called him Tortoise because he taught us.[3]

Ten hours the first day . . . nine the next, and so on . . . That's the reason they're called lessons . . . because they lessen from day to day.[4]

[1] Op. cit., 'The Drop of a Hat', p. 54.
[2] In *The Penguin Book of Comic and Curious Verse*, p. 160.
[3] *Alice*, p. 127.
[4] *Alice*, p. 130.

... no wise fish would go anywhere without a porpoise ... if a
fish came to *me* and told me he was going on a journey, I
should say, 'With what porpoise?'[1]

Thackeray demands that we both hear and see the memoirs of
his 'genlmnly' footman who tells us:

I may be illygitmit . . . but I've always had genlmnly tastes
through life, and have no doubt that I come of genlmnly
origum.[2]

The idiosyncratic spelling of Yellowplush is, in part, a joke made
possible by the gulf between standard English spelling and
pronunciation:

Halgernon was a barrystir . . . he moved in the most xquizzit
suckles . . . and verry glad I was, to be sure, to be a valley to a
zion of the nobillaty.[3]

Yellowplush is also a variation of that hoary old literary game of
satirizing those whose reverence for a social class other than their
own is reflected in the language they use.[4] Thackeray wants us to
laugh at the affectations of the footman and, perhaps, at the
'manners and usitches of genteel society'.[5]

The complicated humour-language of Thurber's *The Wonderful
O* demands our closest possible visual attention. The ear contributes little or nothing. The context of the two quotations which
follow is a situation arising from the desire of a man to eliminate the
letter O because it has unhappy and tragic associations for him.
In the community which he rules, the letter O is removed from the
alphabet and a taboo is imposed on everything with an O in its

[1] *Alice*, p. 137.
[2] W. M. Thackeray, *The Yellowplush Papers and Early Miscellanies* (The
Oxford Thackeray, 1908), p. 168.
[3] *Ibid.*, p. 190.
[4] Cf. Armado, Holofernes, Nathaniel (*Love's Labour's Lost*); Osric (*Hamlet*);
Dogberry (*Much Ado*), etc.
[5] *Yellowplush*, p. 155.

name. Two kinds of humour arise from this theme: one where the linguistic device is dominant and a freak language is produced; the other where both form and meaning have determined the choice of words:

'They are swing chas. What is slid? What is left that's slace? We are begne and webegne. Life is bring and brish. Even schling is flish. Animals in the z are less lacnic than we. Vices are filled with paths and scial intercurse is baths. Let us gird ur lins like lins and rt the hrr and ust the afs.'
    'What nannibickering is this?' cried the blacksmith.
    'What is this gibberish?'
    'English,' said Andreus, 'without its O's.'[1]

They can't play symphonies, or rhapsodies, sonatas or concerti. I'll take away their oratorios and choirs and choruses, and all their soloists, their baritones and tenors and sopranos, their altos and contraltos and accompanists. All they'll have is the funeral march, the chant and anthem, and the dirge, and certain snatches.'[2]

The first of these is almost impossible to read aloud and would certainly lose its point if not seen. The second could be grasped without being seen, but the humour is heightened by visual reading.

Discollocation

My second subdivision of linguistic humour is that where thought acts on or through language. In the first category, which I have called Discollocation, all the examples discussed are characterized by some sort of violation of expectancy. This effect is sometimes achieved by the disruption of any collocation of two or more words which long or frequent association has established as a cliché. The parts are subsequently reassembled, but echoes of the cliché remain in the newly-constructed sense. This happens in Ogden Nash's poem talking about credit facilities extended to the very rich:

[1] Op. cit., p. 103.
[2] Op. cit., p. 91.

... it's very funny
But somehow if you're rich enough you can get away with
spending water like money.[1]

The Goons often achieve their ridiculous deviations from the
normal and hum-drum by shattering the predictability of clichés:

> He flung the interloper aside with a muttered oath, 'I swear to
> tell the truth, the whole truth, and nothing but the truth.'*

At other times they coin their own clichés in what we might
(pompously) call a revival of the oral-formulaic tradition of
stylized epithets. Thus, the Chinese are always 'fiendish', the aged
Minnie Bannister is always called 'modern Min' by her decrepit
paramour who describes her exuberance as 'wicked-sinful'.

The Goons frequently violate expectation by an overlapping of
senses derived from co-existent lexical possibilities. In 'the floods
are rising at the rate of three-and-six an hour'* the association of
both prices and floods with the word 'rising' leads to the unex-
pected—and hence funny—direction which the sentence takes.

Before I leave this category of humour which works through use
or abuse of collocation, I want to mention the parodying of jargon:
specialized language based on the vocational or some other activity
of a given clique. In the following examples, enough concession
to expectation is made to establish the associations required by the
situation. A link is established between the speaker and a given
area of specialized language by the barest minimum of genuine
jargon words or phrases. The rest is achieved by resemblances of
sense (1) or sound (2) or a combination of both (3):

> 1 ... sailing west-nor-east-south. I stood on the pilchard with a
>   spanker blowing through my hair and the salty bloaters spin-
>   ning before the goblets. It's a man's life, I tell ye; a man's
>   life ...!*
>
> 2 Let us get back to that ecstatic Spring of 1887, when all the
>   krill was nabbing in the craw ...*

[1] Op. cit., 'Lines Indited with all the Depravity of Poverty', p. 83.

3 [Of Professor Olliphant's Raspberry Machine]:
Stand by the combustion chamber and wobble the doodler.
Raise the wind-volume and punch the squaggle-nut with the
squinge mallet.*

Ambiguity
In this category we find the manipulation of two or more meanings within a single word or phrase. At its most extreme, ambiguity is entirely split: alternative meanings are severed and the
humour lies somehow in the disruption of communication:

'Now look at the year 1880 —'
'1880? Oh, and I haven't got the dinner on yet!'*

'Who is the owner of PC439?'
'I am.'
'Well, would you come out and move him? He's holding up
the traffic.'*

'Put the brake on, Min.'
'It doesn't suit me, Henry.'*

'Here's a pair of braces for your trouble.'
'What trouble?'
'Your trousers keep falling down.'*

[Neddy Seagoon is a criminal]:
'Give yourself up, Neddy.'
'Give myself up? No! I can't break myself of the habit.'*

. . . Winnie-the-Pooh lived in a forest all by himself under the
name of Sanders.
'What does "under the name" mean?' asked Christopher
Robin.
'It means he had the name over the door in gold letters and
lived under it.'[1]

In another kind of split ambiguity, changes of meaning can
involve changes of word function:

[1] A. A. Milne, *Winnie-the-Pooh* (London, 1926), pp. 2–3. This is an example
of the splitting of one phrase into two separate meanings, but the self-conscious-
ness of it also places it in the same category as the Lewis Carroll quotations on
pp. 118 and 119.

'Can I come too?'
'It's about time you came to.'*

'Finally I fell in a heap on the ground. I've no idea who put it there.'*

'There's plenty of good hiding places in the forest. My Dad used to take me there.'
'What for?'
'A good hiding.'*

'Have you ever seen a comic strip?'
'Only in a Turkish Bath.'*

'I was looking around old second-hand shops for second hands.'*

Each of these examples is characterized by the presence of two meanings which we have to grasp separately. We never lose sight of the alternatives, of course, or the ambiguity wouldn't be funny. Some crossword clues work in the same way, primarily intended as an intellectual exercise perhaps, but often achieving the same sort of humour as the examples from the Goons:

CLUE: You can't drink out of these. SOLUTION: *Hours.*
CLUE: Evading the issue. SOLUTION: *Birth control.*

Precision
Finally, I want to look at humour which is based on the elimination of imprecision and ambiguity in language. Precise thinking and logic dominate this kind of humour. It is often exemplified in Goon humour where an essential element is a hypersensitivity to the seemingly irrational and inconsistent in English usage:

Eccles: Oh! I've broken my leg!
Bloodnock: How did you do that?
Eccles: I got a big hammer, and I went bang.*

Is the humour there based on the apparent paradox of our use of an active, transitive construction, implying volition, for the passive and involuntary experience of a leg getting broken? We are now at the farthest extreme from the category of Ambiguity, where we saw the splitting of words or phrases into alternative meanings. In this category, which I've called Precision, humour is based either on a refusal to permit any flexibility of meaning or an insistence that where a word has two senses they are both present *at the same time*, demanding no modification of the context. A. A. Milne achieves this co-existence in a piece of dialogue on the subject of Eeyore's tail:

> *Pooh:*. . . he was fond of it.
> *Owl:* Fond of it?
> *Pooh:* Attached to it.[1]

Similarly, Lewis Carroll's Mouse is not troubled by ambiguity when he offers a group of wet and shivering creatures some history which is 'the driest thing I know'.[2]

Thurber explores, with whimsical sadness, the imprecision which arises when a word assumes figurative and concrete senses which cannot co-exist like Eeyore's two kinds of attachment to his tail:

> I can feel a thing I cannot touch, and touch a thing I cannot feel. The first is sad and sorry. The second is your heart.[3]

Lewis Carroll satirizes the inexactitudes of idiomatic usage:

> *Alice:* I've had nothing yet . . . so I can't take more.
> *March Hare:* You mean you can't take *less* . . . it's very easy to take *more* than nothing.[4]

> *Caterpillar:* Explain yourself!
> *Alice:* I can't explain *myself*, I'm afraid, sir . . . because I'm not myself, you see.[5]

[1] Ibid., p. 50.
[2] *Alice*, p. 46.
[3] *The 13 Clocks*, p. 40.
[4] *Alice*, p. 101.
[5] *Alice*, p. 67.

The Queen in *Alice* orders that some men should be beheaded. The men run away and hide. When the Queen asks the soldiers 'Are their heads off?' she is satisfied with the answer, 'Their heads are gone'.[1] These examples from Lewis Carroll come close in kind to some of the ambiguities discussed earlier. But here the intention seems to be, as with the Grave-digger in *Hamlet*,[2] to use words as absolutes and to suggest that equivocation can undo us.

Lewis Carroll caricatures the extent to which the relationship between word and referent depends on agreement between users of a given language. The Cheshire Cat calls purring 'growling'. Alice says that she calls it 'purring'. Quite unconcerned, the Cheshire Cat replies, 'Call it what you like'.[3] In the linguistic anarchy of Wonderland, a word is no stable or reliable indication of what is being indicated. The Duchess, for example, says:

> . . . there's a large mustard-mine near here. And the moral of that is—the more there is of mine, the less there is of yours.[4]

Such examples seen singly are funny, but the cumulative effect of Carroll's use of language is sinister and accounts, I am sure, for a great deal of the unease that so many readers experience when reading him:

> Alice felt dreadfully puzzled. The Hatter's remark seemed to her to have no sort of meaning in it, and yet it was certainly English.[5]

In contrast with Carroll's world of vagrant words is the Thurber community where the word actually becomes the thing signified. In the onslaught against the letter O, 'the letter of the law' becomes 'the law of the letter' with such effects as this:

[1] *Alice*, p. 110.
[2] *Hamlet*, V. i. 115 ff.
[3] *Alice*, p. 89.
[4] *Alice*, pp. 121–2.
[5] *Alice*, p. 97.

... farmers could keep their cows if they kept them in herds, for cows in herds are kine or cattle.[1]

Linguistic humour doesn't usually drive us into Alice's predicament—it wouldn't be a source of so much pleasure and delight if it did—but it appears to be a use of language separate from all others. I shall not attempt to define here just what it is that distinguishes it. One important question must precede any such analysis: to what extent is the conciseness and brevity of so many of the examples considered here a twentieth-century attainment?

Certainly the advent of sound radio created an unprecedented demand for language which can be immediately assimilated—in contrast with written language, where the reader can pause, consider and, if necessary, re-read, as in this piece of dialogue from Dickens:

(Martin Chuzzlewit is speaking) '. . . a chief ingredient in my composition is a most determined —'

'Obstinacy?' suggested Tom in perfect good faith.

But the suggestion was not so well received as he had expected: for the young man immediately rejoined with some irritation, 'What a fellow you are, Pinch!'

'I beg your pardon,' said Tom, 'I thought you wanted a word.'

'I didn't want that word,' he rejoined. 'I told you obstinacy was no part of my character, did I not? I was going to say, if you had given me leave, that a chief ingredient in my composition is a most determined firmness.'

'Oh!' cried Tom, screwing up his mouth and nodding. 'Yes, yes, I see!'

'And being firm,' pursued Martin, 'of course I was not going to yield to him or give way by so much as the thousandth part of an inch.'

'No, no,' said Tom.

'On the contrary, the more he urged, the more I was determined to oppose him.'[2]

---

[1] *The Wonderful O*, p. 97.

[2] *Martin Chuzzlewit* (The New Oxford Illustrated Dickens, 1951), pp. 95-6.

Here, in contrast with the swiftness of some of the earlier examples of ambiguity, we are shown, at some length, the use of two words for one sense. It is amusing, but transmitted orally would seem long-winded and laboured.

And yet the word-humour of Shakespeare is often akin to that of many modern writers of radio scripts. In common with them, Shakespeare uses language for the ear and not the leisurely eye. A separate survey might well reveal that most of the categories and kinds of modern linguistic humour can be found in Shakespeare's dialogue. His puns are too well-known to warrant further discussion here.[1] But compare the following:

[Neddy Seagoon refuses to pay his rent]
Creditor: Therefore I shall be forced to distrain upon your furniture.
Neddy Seagoon: You filthy swine!*

Pompey: By this hand, sir, his wife is a more respected person than any of us all.
Elbow: Varlet, thou liest! Thou liest, wicked varlet! The time is yet to come that she was ever respected with man, woman, or child.[2]

It may be, too, that Shakespeare introduces the sort of functional ambiguity seen in the modern examples on page 117 above. Such an interpretation of the following lines would lend a touch of bitter humour in keeping with both the mood and the character of the speaker:

Gloucester: What though I kill'd her husband and her father? The readiest way to make the wench amends Is to become her husband and her father.[3]

[1] E.g. *Julius Caesar*, I. i. 10–24; eight possible puns in fifteen lines of dialogue.
[2] *Measure for Measure*, II. i. 162–6.
[3] *Richard III*, I. i. 154–6; the ambiguity that I am suggesting here involves the reading of the last two words:

a *her* (possessive adjective) *father* (noun), as in line 154.

b *her* (object pronoun) *father* (verb) = to be as a father to her (see O.E.D. Father, *v.* 3).

Perhaps much of the humour of, say, the Goons only seems 'modern' to us because the medium through which it reaches us is a twentieth-century invention. It is likely that for the Elizabethans, as for us, the language that aroused the most laughter was that which most effectively exploited the humorous possibilities inhering in immediately current usage.